Letts

Revise
KS3

Geography

Adam Arnell and Andy Brown

Contents

Geography at Key Stage 3

Introduction to KS3 Geography

This Geography Study Guide has been written specifically to provide complete coverage of the Geography National Curriculum at Key Stage 3.

Key Stage 3 Geography is split into the following four aspects.

Geographical Enquiry and Skills

You will be taught to ask geographical questions, in a logical order. You will need to research and present information, justifying your conclusions. You should consider how other people's values and attitudes affect issues.

You will also learn how to use atlases, globes and maps at a range of scales, as well as drawing your own maps. You will be taught how to present information using graphs and diagrams. You will learn how to collect information by carrying out field work, and by using sources such as the internet.

Knowledge and Understanding of Places

You will be taught the location of places, and how to describe and explain the physical and human features of those places. You will explain how and why places change, and how places are connected to each other.

Knowledge and Understanding of Patterns and Processes

You will learn how to describe and explain physical and human features such as river landforms and cities. You will also describe and explain physical and human processes, such as weathering and migration.

Knowledge and Understanding of Environmental Change and Sustainable Development

You will be taught to describe and explain environmental change, such as deforestation or global climate change. You will also explore the idea of sustainable development – protecting the planet for future generations.

National Curriculum Levels

At the end of Year 9 your teacher will make a judgement about which National Curriculum Level you have reached. They will make their decision based on classwork, homework and exams that you have completed during the year.

At 14 most students are expected to have reached Level 5 or 6, although some students may achieve higher or lower levels.

How to achieve Level 4

You need to show your knowledge, skills and understanding in studies of a range of places and environments at more than one scale and in different parts of the world. You need to suggest geographical questions, and use a range of geographical skills to present information. You need to write using appropriate geographical vocabulary. You need to begin to describe geographical patterns and processes. You need to understand how people can both improve and damage the environment. You must explain your own views and the views that other people hold about an environmental change.

How to achieve Level 5

You need to show your knowledge, skills and understanding in studies of a range of places and environments at more than one scale and in different parts of the world. You need to begin to suggest relevant geographical questions, and use appropriate geographical skills and writing to present information. You need to find information, and suggest conclusions to your investigations. You need to describe, and begin to explain, geographical patterns and processes. You need to suggest explanations for the ways in which human activities cause changes to the environment and the different views people hold about them. You must recognise how people try to manage environments sustainably.

How to achieve Level 6

You need to show your knowledge, skills and understanding in studies of a wide range of places and environments at various scales, from local to global, and in different parts of the world. You need to suggest relevant geographical questions in an appropriate sequence, and use appropriate geographical skills and writing to present information. You need to find information from a range of sources, and suggest sensible conclusions to your investigations. You need to explain geographical patterns and processes. You need to recognise how conflicting demands on the environment may arise and describe and compare different approaches to managing environments. You must appreciate that different values and attitudes, including your own, result in different approaches that have different effects on people and places.

How to achieve Level 7

You need to show your knowledge, skills and understanding in studies of a wide range of places and environments at various scales, from local to global, and in different parts of the world. You need to suggest relevant geographical questions in an appropriate sequence, with only a little help from your teacher. You need to use a wide range of appropriate geographical skills, and writing, to present information. You need to find information from a wide range of sources, and critically evaluate them. You need to present well argued conclusions to your investigations. You need to explain geographical patterns and processes and describe how they are linked. You need to appreciate that the environment in a place and the lives of the people who live there are affected by actions and events in other places. You must recognise that human actions, including your own, may have unintended environmental consequences and that change sometimes leads to conflict. You need to appreciate that considerations of sustainable development affect the planning and management of environments and resources.

How this book will help

Successful study

This book should be used to help you throughout Key Stage 3 to make sure you know and understand the key facts and issues as you go along. You should then be able to use this information to help you answer questions.

Success in school depends on regular planned work over a period of time rather than panic bursts of very hard work just before an examination.

You should regularly develop the habit of reviewing the work you have done in school, and making sure you understand it.

Features in the Study Guide

The book is divided into 12 chapters. They cover all the topics you are required to study at Key Stage 3.

Progress checks

Throughout the book there are Progress Check questions. These are there to help you check what you have learned as you go through the topics in the book. Answers are provided in these panels.

Key points

There are Key Point panels in each topic. These panels draw your attention to important information.

Margin comments

Margin Comments contain advice and guidance which will deepen your understanding.

Practice Questions

At the end of each chapter there are a set of practice questions to test your understanding of the topic. You can find answers to these questions on page 159

1 Geographical enquiry and skills

The topics covered in this chapter are:

- Geographical enquiry
- Ordnance Survey map symbols
- Direction, scale and distance
- Relief
- Grid references
- Graphs and maps
- Drawing skills

After studying this topic you should be able to:

- conduct a geographical enquiry
- recognise Ordnance Survey map symbols
- understand how direction and scale are used on maps
- interpret layer shading and contour lines
- use four- and six-figure grid references
- construct graphs and draw maps
- draw diagrams and field sketches.

1.1 Geographical enquiry

What is a geographical enquiry?

Here is a series of questions that you can adapt to conduct a geographical enquiry.

- What is it?
- Where is it?
- When did it happen?
- How did it happen?
- Why did it happen?
- What were the effects?
- What might happen in the future?
- What do I think about it?
- What can I do about it?
- What do the people involved think about it?
- What can they do about it?

A geographical enquiry does not have to answer all of these questions, but it is important that they are tackled in a logical order.

Key Point

A geographical enquiry is a process of finding answers to geographical questions.

Sources of information

An enquiry should use information from several different sources:

- **The Internet** – a vast source of information – begin with www.georesources.co.uk
- **Books** – try your school library, or join your local library, it's free!
- **TV programmes and video** – television can provide good visual and factual information, e.g. the Discovery Channel.
- **Media** – newspapers often have geographical stories and photos, especially after a natural disaster such as an earthquake.
- **Fieldwork** – the collection of 'first-hand' data outside of the classroom is an important geographical enquiry skill.
- **Questionnaires** – surveys of friends, family or the public can provide useful 'first-hand' data.
- **CD-ROMs** – CD-ROMs such as encyclopaedias are good sources of information. However, never just print out information – you should adapt it for your purpose.
- **Leaflets** – many organisations and companies will send you free information if you write to them and ask.

An enquiry can be presented in many different ways. It might be presented as a report, a letter, a newspaper or magazine article, a leaflet, a talk or even a web page.

Evaluating information

Make sure you evaluate your sources of information.

Check for the following:

- **Bias** – Who has supplied the information?
- **Beliefs** – How do people's values and beliefs affect the quality of the information?
- **Accuracy** – is the information reliable and up-to-date?

Progress Check

1 What is a geographical enquiry?
2 Name three sources of information that could be used in a geographical enquiry.
3 State two things you should check for when evaluating information.

1. A process of finding answers to geographical questions. 2. Internet, books, TV, media, fieldwork, questionnaires, CD-ROMs, leaflets. 3. Bias, beliefs, accuracy.

1.2 Ordnance Survey map symbols

Key Point
Ordnance Survey (OS) is the official organisation responsible for producing maps of Britain.

Ordnance Survey publishes maps at a range of different scales for the whole country. Maps at a scale of 1:50 000 are called Landranger maps. Maps at a scale of 1:25 000 are called Explorer maps.

Symbols

Some symbols are to scale, while others appear much bigger than what they are representing in real life.

Maps need to be clear and easy to read, therefore symbols are used instead of words to show important information. Symbols save space and can be understood by people no matter what language they speak.

Key Point
OS symbols can be divided into a number of different types.

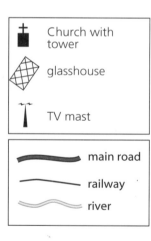

Church with tower

glasshouse

TV mast

main road

railway

river

lake

coniferous wood

park

farmland or countryside

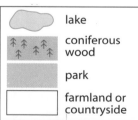

All maps must include a key to explain what the symbols mean.

Small drawings

Some symbols are drawings that look like the thing in real life. For example, a church with a tower, a glasshouse or a lighthouse. Sometimes drawings are used that look nothing like the real thing. For example, a youth hostel, a bus station or a train station.

Lines

Line symbols are used to show things such as roads, railways, rivers and footpaths. Line symbols also show boundaries between counties and areas such as National Parks. **Contour lines** are used to show the height of the land above sea level.

Colours

Coloured areas are used to show large areas of land use. Blue is used to show the sea and lakes. Green, sometimes with drawings, shows woodland and forests. Grey is used to show parks. Pink/orange is used to show buildings. The most common colour on Ordnance Survey maps is white, which represents either farmland or open countryside.

P	post office
PH	public house
MP	milepost

Letters

Capital letters can be used as symbols. For example, 'P' stands for post office, 'PH' stands for public house and 'PC' stands for public convenience (toilet).

Sch	school
cemy	cemetery
Hospl	hospital
Fm	farm

Abbreviations

Words can be shortened to save space. Cemetery is shortened to 'cemy', hospital to 'Hospl' and farm to 'Fm'. These abbreviations are not shown on the map key.

⌂	museum
i	information centre
P	parking

Tourist information

Tourist information symbols are always blue. They show areas that are interesting to visit or places of recreation. They include campsites, museums, preserved railways and theme parks.

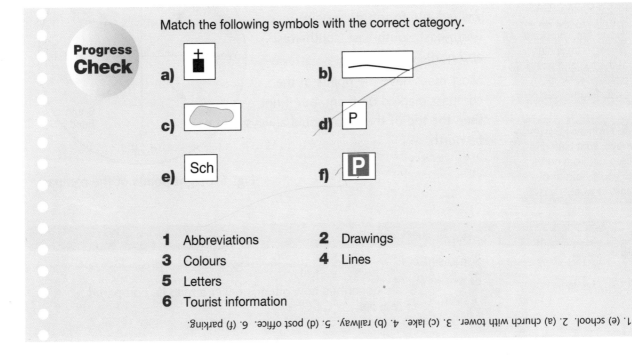

Progress Check

Match the following symbols with the correct category.

a) ✝

b)

c)

d) P

e) Sch

f) P

1	Abbreviations	**2**	Drawings
3	Colours	**4**	Lines
5	Letters		
6	Tourist information		

1. (e) school. 2. (a) church with tower. 3. (c) lake. 4. (b) railway. 5. (d) post office. 6. (f) parking.

1.3 Direction, scale and distance

Direction

> **Key Point**
>
> Direction is used to describe where one place is in relation to another.

One way of remembering the arrangement of the points of a compass is with the saying, 'Never Eat Shredded Wheat' – beginning at the top and going clockwise, North, East, South, West.

On Ordnance Survey maps, light blue grid lines run from north to south, and from east to west.

Direction is given using the points of the compass: north, south, east and west.

The points of a compass can be divided into four further points: north-east, south-east, south-west and north-west.

Most maps have the points of the compass marked on them, but if not, then the top of the map should always be north.

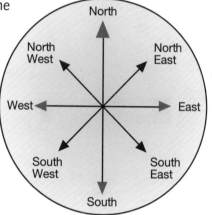

Fig. 1.1 Eight points of the compass.

Scale

> **Key Point**
>
> Scale describes how much smaller a map is, compared to real life.

Ordnance Survey maps always have a scale at the bottom.

A 1:50 000 scale map is 50 000 times smaller than real life. This means that 2 centimetres are equal to 1 kilometre. A 1:25 000 scale map is 25 000 times smaller than real life. Therefore 4 centimetres are equal to 1 kilometre. As the scale increases, the level of detail on the map increases. Remember that whatever the scale of an OS map, the grid squares are always equal to one kilometre.

Distance

> **Key Point**
>
> Maps can be used to measure the distance between places.

The easiest way to measure distance on a map is with a piece of paper.

1 Place a piece of paper on the map, between the two places you want to measure.

2 Mark the two places onto the piece of paper using arrows.

3 Put the piece of paper along the scale at the bottom of the map, with the first arrow at zero.

4 Read off the distance using the scale.

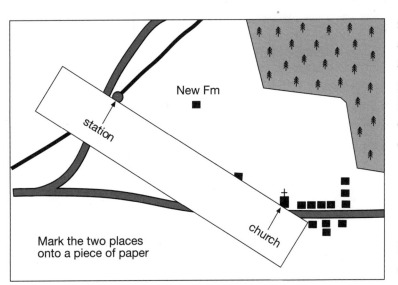

Mark the two places onto a piece of paper

To measure distances that are not in a straight line, the best option is to use a piece of string. If string is not available try marking off a piece of paper in small sections. It is always best to avoid using a ruler because it is easy to make mistakes converting centimetres into kilometres.

Fig 1.2 Measuring distance on a map.

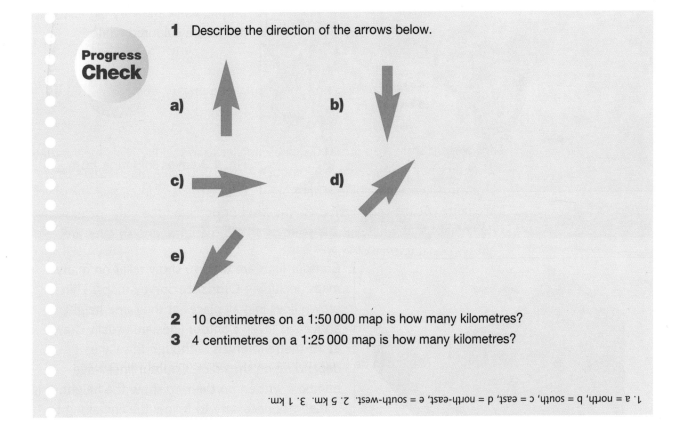

Progress Check

1 Describe the direction of the arrows below.

a)

b)

c)

d)

e)

2 10 centimetres on a 1:50 000 map is how many kilometres?

3 4 centimetres on a 1:25 000 map is how many kilometres?

1. a = north, b = south, c = east, d = north-east, e = south-west. 2. 5 km. 3. 1 km.

1.4 Relief

What is relief?

Key Point

Relief is the height and shape of the land.

The surface of the Earth is rarely flat. Some areas are mountainous with high land and steep slopes. Other areas are low lying with gentle slopes. Since maps are drawn on flat paper, special symbols have to be used to show relief. These symbols include layer colouring, contour lines, spot heights and triangulation points.

Layer colouring

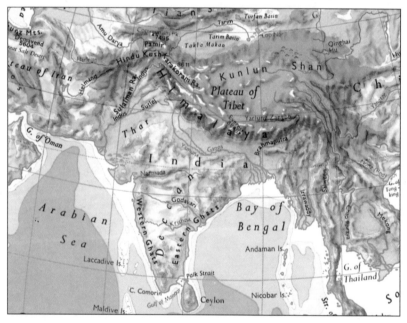

Layer colouring is used mainly for physical maps in atlases. Colours are used to show different heights above sea level. Low land is usually green and high land is brown. Very high mountains are shown in purple, while the very highest points are coloured white.

Fig. 1.3 Layer colouring from a map in an atlas.

Contour lines

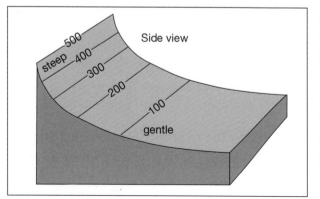

Contour lines are used to show relief on many maps, including Ordnance Survey maps. Thin brown lines join all places at the same height above sea level. Contour lines are usually drawn at 10-metre intervals, although this varies depending on the relief. Contour lines have numbers written on them to show the height. It is sometimes necessary to follow the line along to find the number.

Fig. 1.4 Side view of contour lines.

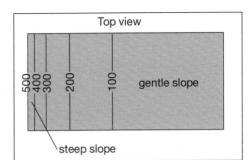

Top view

gentle slope

steep slope

Contour lines are very useful for working out the shape of the land. The simple rule is that the closer together the lines, the steeper the slope. The further apart the lines, the gentler the slope.

Fig. 1.5 Top view of contour lines.

Spot heights and triangulation points

Triangulation points are actually triangular shaped concrete pillars which were used in the past by the Ordnance Survey to make very accurate height measurements.

Some points on an OS map are marked with an exact height in metres. These points are called 'spot heights' or 'triangulation points'. Spot heights are shown by a dot with a number written alongside. Triangulation points are shown as a blue triangle with a dot inside. The height in metres is written alongside.

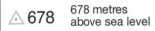

• 364   364 metres above sea level

△ 678   678 metres above sea level

Progress Check

1 What is meant by the word 'relief' in geography?
2 What colour is used to show the highest land when layer colouring is used?
3 What is the usual interval between contour lines on an Ordnance Survey map?
4 What is indicated when contour lines are close together?
5 What is the symbol for a triangulation point?

1. The shape and height of the land. 2. White. 3. 10 metres. 4. Steep slope. 5. ▽

1.5   Grid references

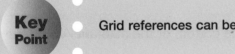

Key Point   Grid references can be used to locate any place in Britain.

Grid references operate at a range of scales.

National grid

Britain is divided into a national grid by the Ordnance Survey. Each grid square covers 100 kilometres x 100 kilometres, and is identified by a two-letter grid reference.

Four-figure grid references

Four-figure grid references locate an area of one km² on an OS map. To find the square described by a four-figure grid reference follow these steps:

1 Move **along the bottom** of the map until you come to the first two numbers.

2 Move **up the side** of the map, until you come to the second two numbers.

3 Follow the two lines until they meet.

This point forms the corner of four grid squares. The correct grid square is the one above, and to the right, of that point.

> Grid lines running up and down a map are called 'eastings'. The lines running across a map are called 'northings'.

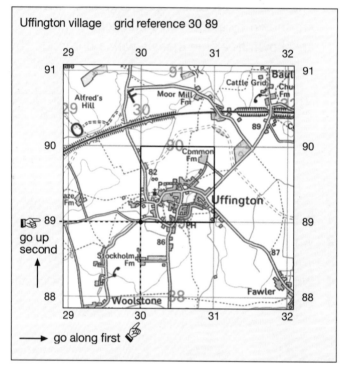

Fig. 1.6 Four-figure grid reference.

Six-figure grid references

Six-figure grid references locate an area of 100 metres² on an Ordnance Survey map. To find the area described by a six-figure grid reference follow these steps:

1 Move along the bottom of the map until you come to the first two numbers.

2 To find the third number, imagine the next square is divided into ten small parts. Move along until you come to about the right place.

3 Move up the side of the map until you find the fourth and fifth numbers.

4 To find the sixth number, again imagine the next square is divided into ten.

5 Follow the two lines until they meet.

> You are allowed to be out by one either way on six-figure grid references.

This point is the exact six-figure grid reference.

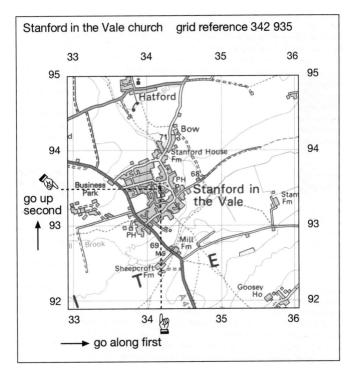

Stanford in the Vale church   grid reference 342 935

go up second ↑

→ go along first

Fig. 1.7 Six-figure grid reference.

Progress
Check

1 Which numbers are at the following grid references?
a) 358948
b) 340930
c) 339943
d) 345935
e) 352923

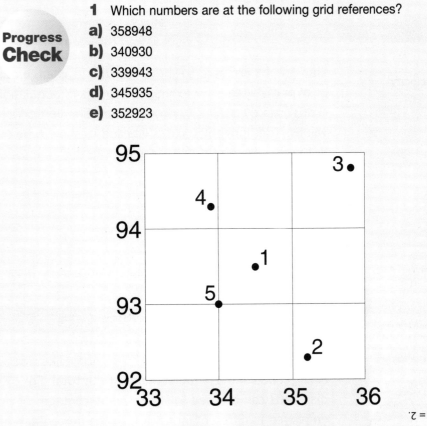

1. a = 3, b = 5, c = 4, d = 1, e = 2.

1.6 Graphs

Bar graphs

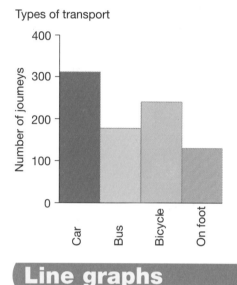

Fig. 1.8 Bar graph.

Bar graphs should be used to show **amounts** of things. They can be used to show one type of data, such as rainfall or pebble sizes. They can also be used to show different types of data, such as types of transport. The vertical axis has a scale to show the number of each item. The horizontal axis is labelled to show the types of data for each bar. If the bars all show the same type of data, such as rainfall, they should all be the same colour. If they show different types of data, they should be different colours.

Line graphs

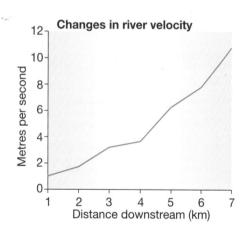

Fig. 1.9 Line graph.

Line graphs are used to show how things **change over time**, or **over distance** – for example, changes in population or changes in river velocity downstream. The vertical axis shows values. The horizontal axis is labelled to show time or distance. Line graphs can include more that one set of data, if different colours are used.

Pie charts

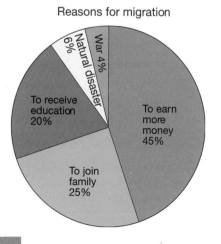

Fig. 1.10 Pie chart.

A pie chart is a circle divided into sections, like slices of pie. Each section shows a **percentage** of the **total**. For example, pie charts can be used to show the percentages of people employed in different industries, or the percentage of ethnic groups in a population. One percent is equal to 3.6 degrees on a pie chart.

Pie charts can only be used to show percentages.

Scatter graphs

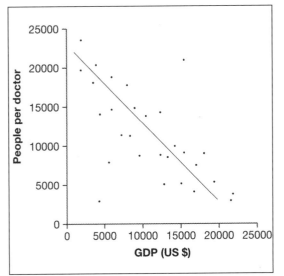

Scatter graphs are used to show **links between two sets of data.** Links can be shown between data such as income and health, or air pressure and wind speed. Scatter graphs have two axes. The scale for the data that causes the change goes along the horizontal axis. The scale for the data that is being changed goes along the vertical axis. Each pair of figures is plotted as a dot, which must not be joined up. The dots make a pattern which shows if there is a link between the data. There may be a positive relationship or a negative relationship. If the dots are random then there may be no relationship.

Fig. 1.11 Scatter graph.

Progress Check

1 Match the following data with the correct type of graph.

a) The percentage of different types of vehicle.

b) Changes in energy use over a decade.

c) Relationship between Gross National Product and life expectancy.

d) Average wages in five different countries.

line graph   bar graph   scatter graph   pie chart

1. (a) pie chart, (b) line graph, (c) scatter graph, (d) bar graph.

1.7   Maps

Key Point

Maps are often used in geography to display data.

Choropleth maps

Choropleth maps use shading to show **differences between areas** – for example, standards of living and climate. Data is divided into between three and nine groups. The divisions do not have to be equal, but no value must appear in more than one group. Groups might be, for example, 1 to 4.9, 5 to 9.9, etc. A base map is divided into different areas and then coloured or shaded to show different values. Darker colours should be used to show higher values. A key is used to show the value of each colour.

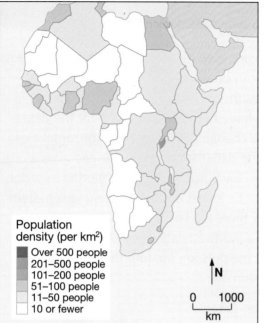

Fig. 1.12 Choropleth map.

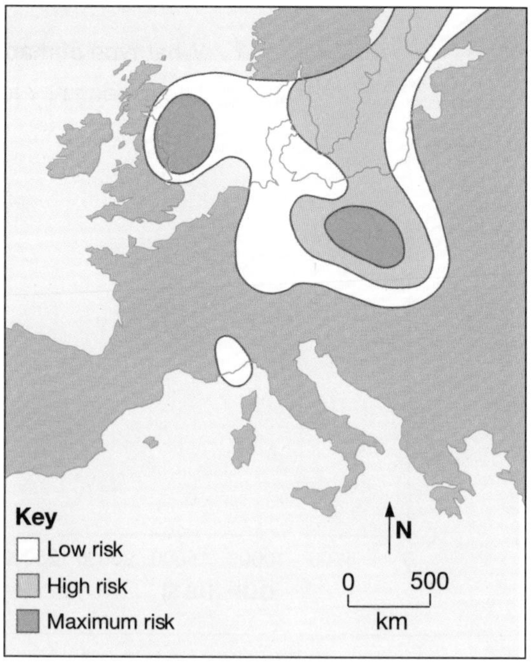

Fig. 1.13 Isoline map.

Isoline maps

Isoline maps use lines to join up places of the same value. They are used to show data such as height, air pressure, temperature and rainfall. Isolines must never cross over each other. The space between the isolines can be shaded. The higher the value, the darker the shading.

Flow line maps

Flow line maps use lines of different widths to show the value of data. They are useful for showing data such as traffic flows and movements of migrants. Arrow lines are drawn onto a base map to show the direction of movement. The width of each line depends on the value of the data.

Remember to include a key where necessary.

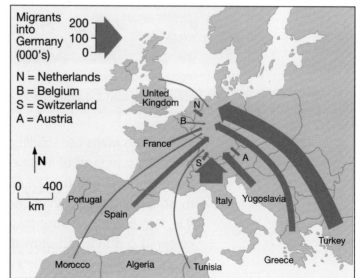

Fig. 1.14 Flow line map.

Progress Check

1 What type of map would you draw to show the following?
a) Life expectancy for all countries in South America
b) The destination of the UK's exports
c) Air pressure

1. (a) choropleth, (b) flow line, (c) isoline.

1.8 Drawing skills

Key Point

Being able to draw sketch maps, diagrams and field sketches are important geographical skills.

Fig. 1.15 Sketch map.

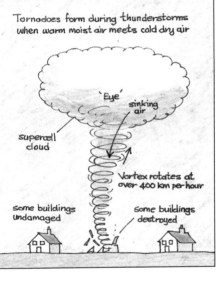

Fig. 1.16 Diagram.

Sketch maps

Sketch maps are drawn freehand, rather than being traced. A sketch map is better than a photocopied map because it allows you to include only the detail you need. Maps should be drawn in pencil and labelled neatly in pen. Sketch maps must always include a scale and a compass direction. The map should be given a suitable title and surrounded with a border. Colour and a key can be added if needed.

Diagrams

Diagrams are used to present information graphically. Diagrams do not need to be artistic but should be neat. Always draw diagrams in pencil and label them in pen. Leave room around diagrams to add labels. Guidelines should be used to connect labels with the diagram. When the diagram is finished it should be given a title, and a border drawn around it.

Field sketches

A field sketch is a labelled drawing of geographical features. Field sketches allow features to be described and explained in much more detail than writing alone. They can also be labelled during fieldwork, while photos require you to wait for them to be developed or printed. A field sketch should only include things relevant to the topic. Field sketches must include a title, a grid reference, a direction and a date.

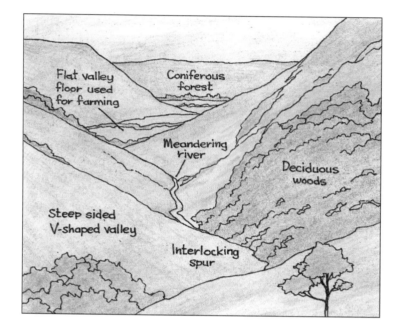

Flat valley floor used for farming
Coniferous forest
Meandering river
Deciduous woods
Steep sided V-shaped valley
Interlocking spur

Fig. 1.17 Field sketch.
Grid reference: 123101
Direction: North East
Date: 19 August 2003

Progress Check

1 Draw a field sketch of the photo below.

Practice questions

1 What is the name of the organisation responsible for producing maps of the United Kingdom? **(1)**

2 Name the following OS map symbols. **(6)**

a) 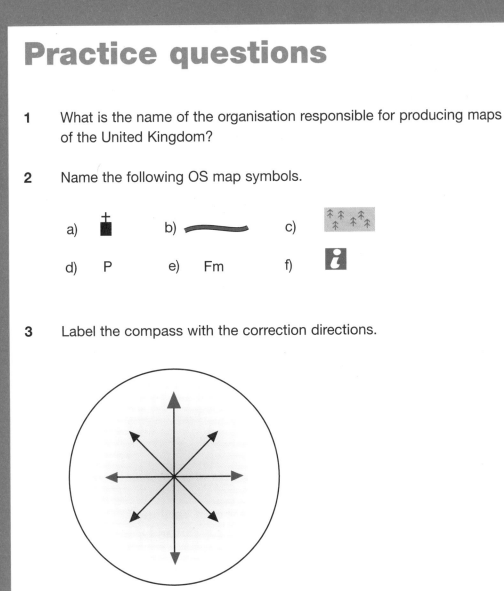   b)   c)

d)   P   e)   Fm   f)

3 Label the compass with the correction directions. **(8)**

4 Draw a contour map of this island. **(3)**

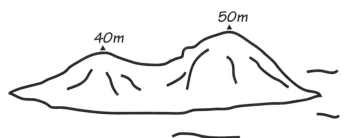

5 Give the six-figure grid references of points A, B and C. **(3)**

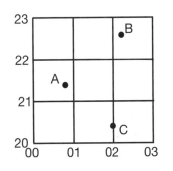

2 Tectonic processes

After studying this topic you should be able to:

- describe the structure of the Earth
- explain how tectonic plates move
- describe the different types of plate boundary
- describe the different types of volcano
- describe and explain the causes and effects of a volcanic eruption
- explain what causes earthquakes
- describe and explain the causes and effects of earthquakes
- explain how volcanic eruptions and earthquakes can be predicted.

2.1 The Earth

The Earth is one of nine planets in our solar system. It was formed 4.6 billion years ago from matter which was created in the 'Big Bang'. Over time the outside of the Earth cooled to form a solid rock surface, but the Earth's interior remains extremely hot.

The structure of the Earth

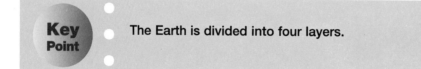

Key Point The Earth is divided into four layers.

- The **crust** is a layer of solid rock which is between 5 km and 90 km thick. It is thinnest under the sea, and thickest on the continents.
- The **mantle** is a 2900 km layer of semi-solid rock. The temperature of the mantle is up to 5000°C. The mantle is hot enough to melt, but is kept solid by the huge pressure from the rock above.

Movements of liquid metal in the outer core are thought to cause the Earth's magnetic field.

The temperature at the Earth's core is the same as the surface of the sun.

- The **outer core** is made of liquid iron and nickel. It is 2100 km thick, and reaches temperatures of over 5000°C.
- The **inner core** is a solid ball of iron and nickel. It has a diameter of 2800 km, and is thought to be as hot as 5500°C.

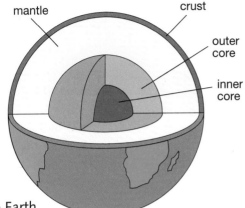

Fig. 2.1 The structure of the Earth.

Tectonic plates

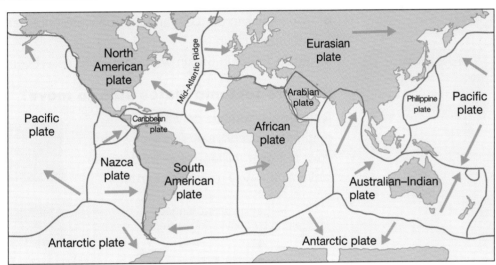

Fig. 2.2 Earth's tectonic plates.

The Earth's crust is broken into huge slabs of rock called **tectonic plates**. There are seven major plates and twelve smaller ones.

There are two different types of plate:

Continental	Relatively light (less dense)	Cannot sink into the mantle	Forms the land
Oceanic	Relatively heavy (more dense)	Can sink into the mantle and be destroyed	Forms the sea bed

Progress Check

1 When was the Earth formed?
2 How thick is the Earth's crust?
3 What is the temperature of the Earth's core?
4 What is the Earth's core made from?
5 Which type of tectonic plate can be destroyed in the mantle?

1. 4.6 billion years ago. 2. Between 5 and 90 km thick. 3. 5500°C. 4. iron and nickel.
5. Oceanic.

2.2 Continental drift

Moving continents

In the past, all the world's continental plates were joined together, forming a super-continent. Two hundred million years ago the super-continent broke up into separate continents and began to drift very slowly around the Earth's surface. If you look carefully at a world map today you can see how the continents would fit together like a jigsaw puzzle.

Other evidence for continental drift:

- Identical fossils of a small reptile have been found in Africa and South America.
- Mountains in the USA and Europe were once part of one large mountain chain.
- Rocks found in Britain were formed in desert conditions.

> Continental drift is still happening today.

> Tectonic plates move at about the same speed as your fingernails grow.

How are tectonic plates able to move?

Tectonic plates move only a few centimetres every year. This seems very slow, but over millions of years they can move all the way round the Earth.

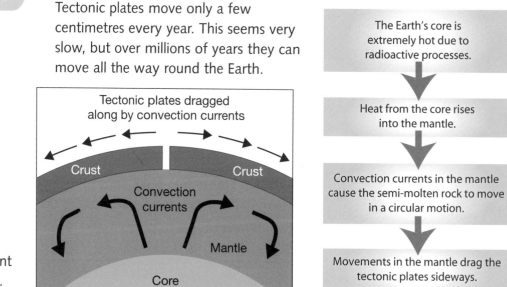

Fig. 2.3 Movement of tectonic plates.

The Earth's core is extremely hot due to radioactive processes.

↓

Heat from the core rises into the mantle.

↓

Convection currents in the mantle cause the semi-molten rock to move in a circular motion.

↓

Movements in the mantle drag the tectonic plates sideways.

> **Key Point**
>
> The movement of the Earth's tectonic plates is responsible for earthquakes and volcanic eruptions.

Progress Check

True or false?

1 The Earth's continents used to be joined together.

2 Mountains in Australia and the USA were once part of a large mountain chain.

3 Britain used to be a desert.

4 Tectonic plates are no longer moving around the world.

1. True. 2. False. 3. True. 4. False.

2.3 Tectonic plate boundaries

Plate boundaries are the places where the edges of two or more tectonic plates meet.

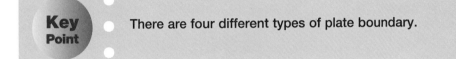

Key Point ● There are four different types of plate boundary.

Constructive boundary

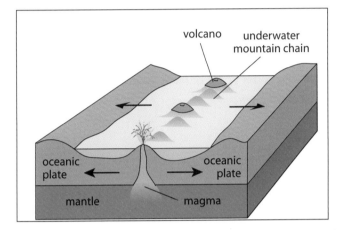

● Oceanic plates **move apart**.
● Lava erupts.
● New crust is formed on the sea bed.
● Underwater volcanoes.
● Gentle earthquakes.

Fig. 2.4 Constructive boundary.

Destructive boundary

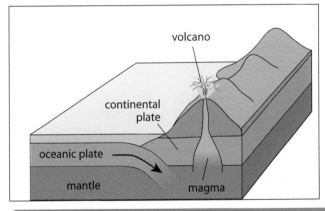

● Oceanic and continental plates **move together**.
● Heavier oceanic crust is pushed down into the mantle.
● Ocean crust is melted and destroyed.
● Explosive volcanoes.
● Violent earthquakes.
● Most hazardous boundaries.

Fig. 2.5 Destructive boundary.

Collision boundary

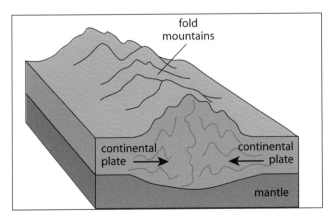

● Continental plates **move together**.
● Plates are too 'light' to sink into the mantle.
● Plates buckle and fold to form mountains.
● Volcanic activity is rare.
● Violent earthquakes.

Fig. 2.6 Collision boundary.

Conservative boundary

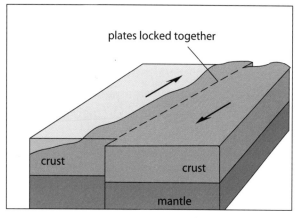

- Tectonic plates move in different directions, or at different speeds.
- Plates are locked together by friction.
- Pressure builds up until a plate breaks along a fault line.
- No volcanoes.
- Violent earthquakes.

Fig. 2.7 Conservative boundary.

Progress Check

Match the following statements with the correct type of plate boundary.

1 Two plates move sideways past each other.
2 Oceanic plates move apart.
3 Continental plates move together.
4 Oceanic and continental plates move together.

a) Constructive
b) Destructive
c) Collision
d) Conservative

1. = (d). 2. = (a). 3. = (c). 4. = (b)

2.4 Volcanoes

Key Point

A volcano is a mountain formed from eruptions of lava (molten rock) and ash.

Volcanoes can be classified as active, dormant or extinct.

- **Active** – has erupted recently and is expected to erupt again in the future.
- **Dormant** – presently inactive, but may erupt in the future.
- **Extinct** – has not erupted in the past few thousand years and is not expected to erupt in the future.

There are 1500 volcanoes around the world, but few are erupting at any one time.

Types of volcano

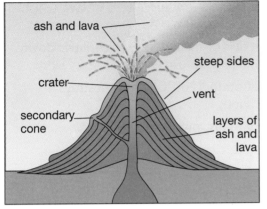

There are a variety of different types of volcano.

Composite volcanoes

Composite volcanoes are high with steep sides. They are formed by alternate eruptions of ash and thick, sticky lava. Composite volcanoes can erupt extremely violently.

Example: Mt St Helens, USA.

Fig. 2.8 Composite volcano.

Shield volcanoes

Shield volcanoes are wide with gently sloping sides. They are formed from eruptions of thin, runny lava which is able to flow a long way before it cools and becomes solid rock.

Example: Mauna Loa, Hawaii.

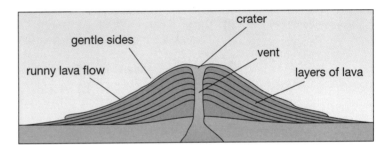

Fig. 2.9 Shield volcano.

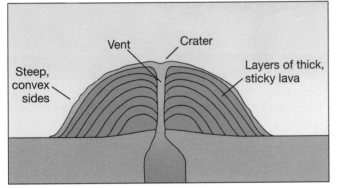

Fig. 2.10 Dome volcano.

Dome volcanoes

Dome volcanoes have steep convex sides. They are formed from eruptions of thick, sticky lava which cools before it is able to flow very far.

Example: Mont Pelée, Martinique.

Ash volcanoes

Ash volcanoes are cones with steep concave sides. Ash and cinders are erupted into the air, and then fall back to Earth where they pile up in layers.

Example: Paricutín, Mexico.

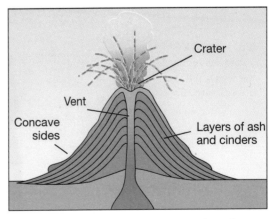

Fig. 2.11 Ash volcano.

Effects of volcanic eruptions

The pyroclastic flow which occurred when Mt St Helens erupted (1980) flattened trees up to 25 km away from the volcano.

- **Pyroclastic flow** – cloud of red hot gas, ash and pieces of lava which travels at over 120 mph.
- **Mudflow** – mixture of ash with rain or melted ice, which flows down the side of a volcano.
- **Lava flow** – river of molten rock up to 1200°C, which destroys everything in its path.
- **Ash fall** – layers of ash can bury roads, buildings and crops.

Progress Check

1 A volcano that is not expected to erupt again is described as _____.
a) dead   **b)** dormant   **c)** extinct

2 There are _____ volcanoes around the world.
a) 1000   **b)** 1500   **c)** 3000

3 A _____ volcano is wide with gently sloping sides.
a) dome   **b)** shield   **c)** ash

1. = (c). 2. = (b). 3. = (b).

2.5   Mount Nyiragongo

Location

Mount Nyiragongo is a 3469-metre-high volcano in the Democratic Republic of Congo, Africa.

Key Point

The eruption of Mount Nyiragongo is an example of a volcanic eruption in a Less Economically Developed Country (LEDC).

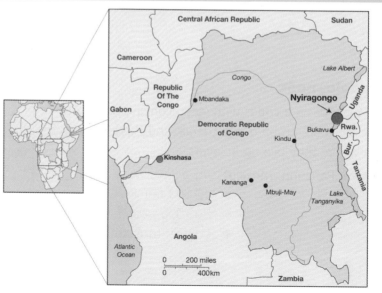

Fig. 2.12 Location map for Mount Nyiragongo.

Eruption

Mount Nyiragongo erupted on 17 January 2002. Three slow-moving rivers of lava flowed down the sides of the volcano, destroying 14 villages. One of the lava flows travelled for over 10 km, passing through the city of Goma, before stopping at Lake Kivu.

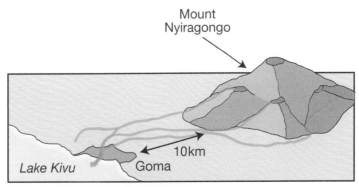

Fig. 2.13 The eruption.

Cause

Mount Nyiragongo is a composite volcano, made of layers of ash and lava.

Mount Nyiragongo is one of a chain of volcanoes situated along the East African Rift Valley. Here the Earth's crust has fractured, and the land has dropped down to form a 4000 km long valley. In places, lava is able to reach the surface through cracks in the rock. Where lava escapes, volcanoes such as Mount Nyiragongo have formed.

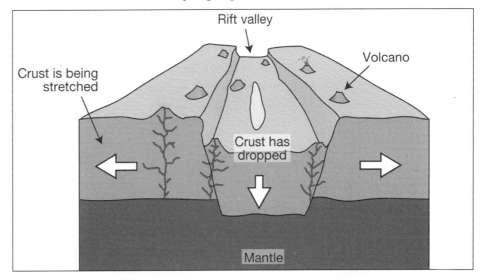

Fig. 2.14
East African rift valley.

Impacts

- Streams of lava flowed across the runway at Goma airport and set light to aviation fuel.
- A 50 metre wide lava flow passed through Goma and destroyed 300 buildings.
- 45 people were killed.
- 12 000 families were made homeless.
- 300 000 people fled to safety in Rwanda.
- Looters took advantage of the confusion to rob shops and homes.

Mount Nyiragongo is one of Africa's most active volcanoes.

Progress
Check

Cross out the incorrect words in the sentences below.
1 Mount Nyiragongo is a volcano in <u>Asia/Africa</u>.
2 The eruption of Mount Nyiragongo destroyed 14 <u>towns/villages</u>.
3 Mount Nyiragongo's lava flow stopped when it reached <u>Lake Kivu/Lake Victoria</u>.
4 In the town of Goma <u>300/3000</u> buildings were destroyed by the lava flow.

Incorrect words: 1. Asia. 2. towns. 3. Lake Victoria. 4. 3000.

2.6 Earthquakes

> **Key Point**
>
> There are approximately 6000 earthquakes every year in the world. Only a few are powerful enough to cause significant damage.

What causes earthquakes?

Earthquakes happen mainly in areas which are on tectonic plate boundaries.

The place underground where the rock breaks is known as the **focus**. The place at the surface, directly above the focus, is called the **epicentre**. Seismic waves ripple outwards from the epicentre in all directions.

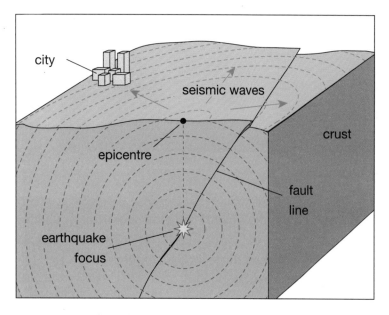

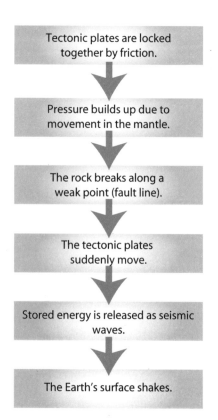

Tectonic plates are locked together by friction.

↓

Pressure builds up due to movement in the mantle.

↓

The rock breaks along a weak point (fault line).

↓

The tectonic plates suddenly move.

↓

Stored energy is released as seismic waves.

↓

The Earth's surface shakes.

Fig. 2.15 Earthquake focus and epicentre.

Impacts of earthquakes

- **Structural damage**

Structures that have not been built to withstand earthquakes may collapse within the first few minutes of an earthquake. Houses, offices blocks and bridges are at risk, and people may be trapped or crushed.

- **Falling objects**

Injuries resulting from falling objects are common. Falling glass from broken windows, and electricity cables, are especially dangerous.

- **Fire**

Gas pipes that have been broken during the earthquake may catch fire. The fires are difficult to put out as the emergency services are overwhelmed and water pipes may also have been broken.

- **Tsunamis**

An earthquake occurring at sea can result in 40 metre high waves, which travel at over 300 mph. Settlements in coastal areas may be wiped out.

- **Disease**

A lack of clean water can result in the spread of disease after a few days. Cholera and typhoid may result in deaths.

- **Economy**

Impacts may be short term or long term.

Earthquakes have a long-term economic impact as individuals, companies and governments have to spend money on rebuilding.

Recording earthquakes

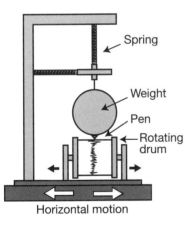

Spring

Weight

Pen

Rotating drum

Horizontal motion

Earthquakes are recorded using very sensitive instruments called **seismometers**. The vibrations they detect are drawn on a **seismograph**. The strength of an earthquake is usually described using the **Richter Scale**. The Richter Scale measures the total amount of energy released in the earthquake. Each level on the Richter Scale is ten times more powerful than the previous one.

Earthquakes are also measured using the Mercalli Scale. The Mercalli Scale measures the amount of damage caused by the earthquake.

Fig. 2.16 Seismometer.

Progress Check

Put the following statements in order to explain how earthquakes happen.

1 The Earth's surface shakes.
2 Tectonic plates are locked together by friction.
3 The tectonic plates suddenly move.
4 Pressure builds up due to movement in the mantle.
5 The rock breaks along a weak point (fault line).
6 Stored energy is released as seismic waves.

2, 4, 5, 3, 6, 1

2.7 The Kobe earthquake

Location

Kobe is an industrial city on the Japanese island of Honshu.

 Key Point

The events in Kobe are an example of an earthquake in a More Economically Developed Country (MEDC).

Earthquake

At 5.46 am on 17 January 1995, an earthquake measuring 7.2 on the Richter Scale occurred in southern Japan. The epicentre of the earthquake was Awaji island, just off the coast of Kobe. The shaking caused by the earthquake lasted for 20 seconds.

Cause

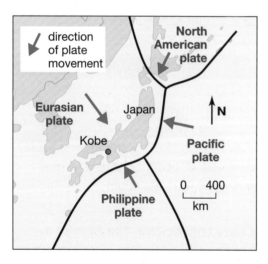

Japan is at risk from earthquakes because it is on a destructive plate boundary. The Pacific plate is moving west and being forced underneath the North American and Philippine plates. Prior to the earthquake, pressure had built up over many years, until finally part of the crust snapped along a fault line. The energy that was released travelled outwards from Awaji island, causing huge damage to Kobe and other cities in the area.

Fig. 2.17 Tectonic plate boundaries affecting Japan.

Impacts

The cost of the Kobe Earthquake was estimated at £80 billion.

More people would have been killed and injured if the earthquake had happened later in the day, as most people were still in bed.

Impacts of the earthquake:
- Older wooden buildings collapsed because of their heavy tile roofs.
- Tall concrete buildings collapsed as the walls gave way.
- Buildings sank into the ground as the soil acted like a liquid.
- Fires were caused by leaking gas pipes.
- 4569 people were killed.
- 14 679 people were injured.
- 190 000 buildings were damaged or destroyed.
- 300 000 people were made homeless.

Progress Check

1 Where is Kobe?
2 What was the strength of the earthquake that struck Kobe in 1995?
3 How long did the earthquake last?
4 What caused the earthquake?
5 What was the estimated cost of the earthquake?

1. Japan. 2. 7.2 on the Richter Scale. 3. 20 seconds. 4. Japan is on a destructive plate boundary. 5. £80 billion.

2.8 Predicting earthquakes and volcanic eruptions

Key Point

The world's population is increasing, and therefore more people are living in areas at risk from earthquakes and volcanoes. It is important to try to predict events, and then prepare for them.

Predicting earthquakes

Predicting earthquakes has proved to be very difficult. Scientists have a good idea of where earthquakes may happen, but not when.

Earthquake prediction methods:

- **Mapping** The locations of previous earthquakes are marked onto a map. Areas that have not had an earthquake for a long period of time are likely to be more at risk.
- **Foreshocks** A series of small tremors may indicate that a larger earthquake will follow.
- **Water levels** A change in water levels caused by movements in the crust may warn of an earthquake.
- **Animals** There is some evidence that animals are aware that earthquakes are going to happen. There are reports from China and Japan that fish, rats and pigs have been seen behaving strangely just before an earthquake.

Preparing for earthquakes

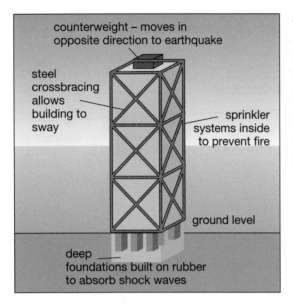

A lot can be done to prepare before an earthquake strikes. Structures can be built to withstand extreme shaking, but this is very expensive. In poorer areas houses should be built from wood as this is more flexible than concrete or bricks.

Other preparation measures include teaching people what to do in the event of an earthquake. In Japan there is a national emergency drill once a year.

Fig. 2.18 An earthquake-proof building.

Predicting volcanic eruptions

Volcanoes can be monitored very closely and it is now possible to give warnings of when they are likely to erupt.

Volcano monitoring methods:
- **Satellite images** are used to monitor the shape and temperature of volcanoes.
- **Gas detectors** placed on the volcano record the amount of sulphur dioxide and carbon dioxide in the air.
- **Seismometers** record earthquakes, which occur as the volcano fills with magma.

Preparing for volcanic eruptions

When a volcanic eruption is predicted a hazard map is produced to show the areas at greatest risk. People living in these areas can then be evacuated. However, the hazard maps are not always accurate. When Mt St Helens erupted in 1980 a number of people were killed in areas that were thought to be safe.

Although it is not possible to stop a volcano from erupting, in some cases lava flows have been diverted. In Iceland, lava flows which threatened a town were halted by spraying them with sea water.

Progress Check

True or false?

1 It is possible to predict the location of earthquakes.

2 It is possible to predict the time of earthquakes.

3 It is possible to predict volcanic eruptions.

1. True. 2. False. 3. True.

Practice questions

1   Name the parts of the Earth shown in the diagram below.   **(4)**

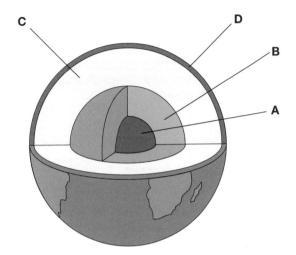

2   Give three pieces of evidence for the process of continental drift.   **(3)**

3   Describe how tectonic plates are able to move.   **(4)**

4   Name the types of volcano shown below.   **(4)**

A
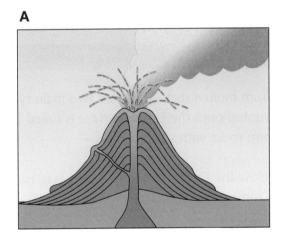

B
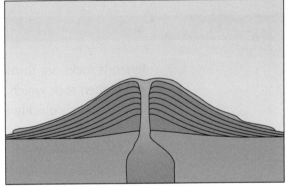

C
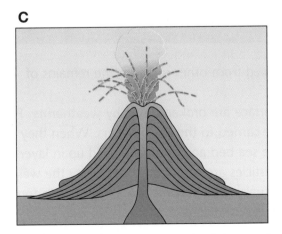

D
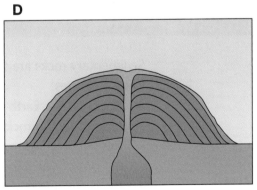

3 Geomorphological processes

The topics covered in this chapter are:

- Rocks and weathering
- Erosion
- River and coastal landscapes
- Hazards

After studying this topic you should be able to:

- describe how rocks are formed
- explain how rocks are broken down by the weather
- explain how rocks are worn away by wind, rivers, ice and the sea
- describe and explain the formation of river landforms
- describe and explain the formation of coastal landforms
- understand the causes and effects of mega-tsunamis.

3.1 Rocks

Key Point

Rocks can be classified into three groups.

Igneous rocks

Igneous rocks are formed from molten rock. There are two main types:

- Molten rock which is erupted onto the Earth's surface is called lava. Lava cools quickly to form rocks with small crystals. Example: basalt.
- Molten rock which is below the Earth's surface is called magma. Magma cools slowly to form rocks with large crystals. Example: granite.

Sedimentary rocks

Sedimentary rocks are formed from other rocks, or the remains of living creatures.

- Rocks on the Earth's surface are broken down by weathering. Particles of worn-down rock are carried to the sea by rivers. When they reach the sea they sink to the sea bed and gradually build up in layers. Over millions of years the particles are squashed together by the weight of the layers above. Eventually they become stuck together to form new rock. Examples: sandstone and clay.

Sedimentary rocks are formed in layers, and often contain fossils.

- The shells and skeletons of dead sea creatures sink to the sea bed. They build up in layers and are compressed together. Again, over millions of years they are cemented together and form new sedimentary rocks. Examples: chalk and limestone.

Metamorphic rocks

Metamorphic rocks are formed from other rocks as a result of volcanic activity or extreme pressure.

Metamorphic rock can be formed from both igneous and sedimentary rocks.

- Rocks which come into contact with magma are heated and changed into other types of rock.
  Examples: limestone becomes marble, sandstone becomes quartzite.
- Extreme pressure caused by tectonic movements can also alter rocks.
  Example: clay becomes slate.

Progress Check

1 Tick the correct category for the following rocks.

	Igneous	Sedimentary	Metamorphic
Marble			
Granite			
Sandstone			
Basalt			
Chalk			
Slate			

Igneous = granite, basalt. Sedimentary = sandstone, chalk. Metamorphic = marble, slate.

3.2 Weathering

Key Point
Weathering is the natural breakdown of rocks at the Earth's surface.

Weathering can be divided into physical, chemical and biological processes.

Physical weathering

Physical weathering happens when the weather breaks down rocks without altering them chemically. Two key types are freeze-thaw weathering and onion-skin weathering.

Freeze-thaw weathering

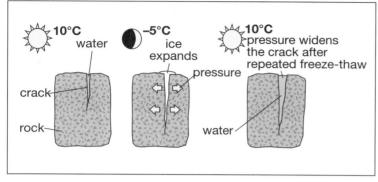

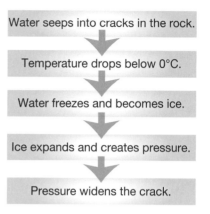

Water seeps into cracks in the rock.

Temperature drops below 0°C.

Water freezes and becomes ice.

Ice expands and creates pressure.

Pressure widens the crack.

Fig. 3.1 Freeze-thaw weathering.

Onion-skin weathering

Onion-skin weathering happens in hot environments.

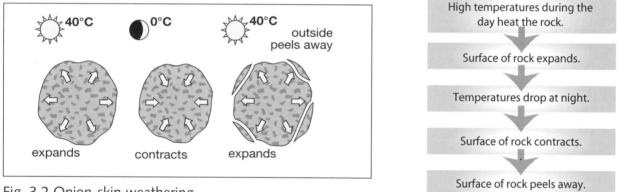

High temperatures during the day heat the rock.

Surface of rock expands.

Temperatures drop at night.

Surface of rock contracts.

Surface of rock peels away.

Fig. 3.2 Onion-skin weathering.

Chemical weathering

Chemical weathering of buildings is a growing problem in cities as air pollution from vehicles and power stations is making rainwater more acidic.

Chemical weathering involves chemical reactions between rainwater and rocks.

Chalk and limestone are made from **calcium carbonate**, which reacts with weak acid. Rainwater is naturally slightly acidic and is able to dissolve these types of rock, especially along cracks or joints.

Biological weathering

Rocks are broken up by a combination of weathering processes, rather than just one.

Biological weathering is the breakdown of rocks by plants, animals and insects.

- Roots from trees and plants grow into cracks in rock. The pressure from expanding roots widens the cracks and breaks up the rock.
- Creatures that burrow or live underground, such as rabbits and worms, help to break up softer rocks such as clay.

Progress Check

1 Name the three categories of weathering.
2 Arrange the following statements in the correct order to explain freeze-thaw weathering.
a) Ice expands.
b) Ice melts.
c) Water seeps into crack.
d) Pressure enlarges crack.
e) Water freezes.

1. Physical, chemical and biological. 2. (c), (e), (a), (d), (b).

3.3 Erosion

Key Point

Erosion is the wearing away of the land by wind, rivers, sea and ice.

Weathering breaks down rocks in one place. Erosion wears away rocks and removes the loose particles.

Wind

In deserts, winds pick up particles of sand and blast them against exposed rocks. Rocks are slowly worn away by **abrasion**, and sculpted into amazing shapes. In desert countries, such as Saudi Arabia, cars have to be protected from sand blasting otherwise all their paint can be stripped away.

Rivers

Rivers erode the land as they flow from their source towards the sea. Pieces of rock break away due to **hydraulic action**, and then wear away the bed and banks by abrasion. The pieces of rock also wear each other down by **attrition**. The greatest erosion takes place when the river is at its maximum flow.

Sea

The sea erodes the coast by wave action. Waves smash into cliffs and break off pieces of rock by hydraulic action. The broken pieces of rock are then picked up by waves and hurled at the cliffs, wearing them away even more. The rock pieces also crash into each other and are worn down by attrition. Coastal erosion is at its maximum during storm conditions.

Ice

Fig. 3.3 A glacier.

Glaciers are rivers of ice which form in cold mountainous areas. Ice freezes around loose blocks of rock and plucks them away as it moves forwards. The blocks of rock which have become embedded in the glacier now grind away the glacier's valley by abrasion. Glaciers are the most powerful agents of erosion.

Processes of erosion

Abrasion	Particles of rock carried by rivers, waves, glaciers and wind rub against, and wear away, the surface of other rocks.
Attrition	Particles of rock grind against each other, becoming smaller, smoother and rounder, as they are carried by wind, rivers, sea and ice.
Hydraulic action	Particles of rock are broken away and removed by the power of moving water in rivers and the sea.
Plucking	As a glacier slides past loose rocks it freezes around them and pulls them away.

Progress Check

1 What are the four agents of erosion?

2 Match the descriptions with the correct type of erosion.

a) Particles of rock are worn away by the power of moving water.

b) Particles of rock wear away the surface of other rocks.

c) Particles of rock are pulled away by ice.

d) Particles of rock bump together and become smoother.

abrasion   attrition   hydraulic action   plucking

1. Wind, rivers, sea and ice. (a) = hydraulic action, (b) = abrasion, (c) = plucking, (d) = attrition.

3.4 River landscapes

Key Point

As rivers flow from high land to low land they shape the Earth's surface by a combination of erosion and deposition to form a number of distinctive landforms.

River basins

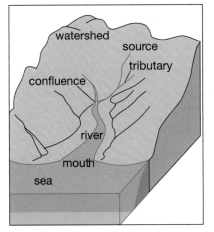

An area of land containing a river and its tributaries is called a river basin. The area of high land which separates two drainage basins is called a **watershed**.

The place where a river begins is called the **source**. Rivers flow downhill from their source to their mouth, at the sea or a lake. During this journey the main river is joined by other rivers called **tributaries**. The point where a tributary joins the river is called a **confluence**. As more water enters the river it becomes wider, deeper and faster flowing.

Fig. 3.4 River basin.

V-shaped valleys

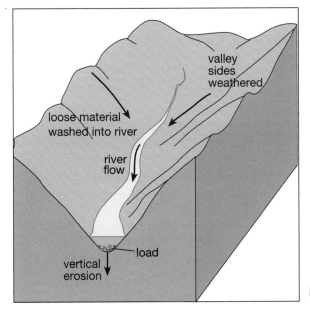

River valleys in upland areas are steep-sided and narrow. They are known as V-shaped valleys because they form the shape of the letter V. They are formed as a river erodes downwards, leaving steep valley sides. The valley sides are slowly weathered and loose material is washed into the river by rainfall. The river transports this material downstream as part of its **load**. The river's load in upland areas contains large rough rocks and boulders. This is because they have not yet been eroded by attrition.

In upland areas the river can look rough and fast flowing, but in fact, rocks and boulders slow the river down.

Fig. 3.5 V-shaped valley.

Waterfalls

Waterfalls form where there is a band of harder rock lying on top of softer rock. The river erodes the softer rock more quickly than the hard rock. This forms a 'step' in the river, where the water falls vertically. At the base of the waterfall, the softer rock is worn away, undercutting the harder rock.

This forms an overhang. Eventually the overhang collapses under its own weight.

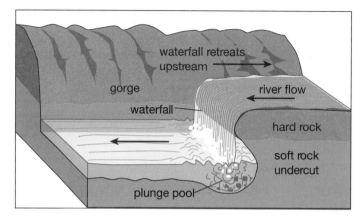

Loose rocks at the base of a waterfall are swirled around by the falling water to erode a plunge pool.

Fig. 3.6 Waterfall.

Each time the rock overhang collapses, the waterfall retreats slightly up the valley. Over many years a steep-sided valley, called a **gorge**, will be created downstream of the waterfall.

Meanders

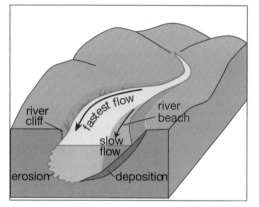

Rivers begin to bend from side to side in upland areas. When they reach lowland areas, the curves can become very large. These curves are known as **meanders**.

The river's flow is fastest on the outside bend of a meander, which is eroded and undercut to form a **river cliff**. On the inside bend, the river flows slowly and deposits material. The material builds up to form an area of shallow land, called a **river beach**.

Fig. 3.7 Meander.

Ox-bow lakes

Ox-bow lakes are horseshoe-shaped lakes, found next to rivers. They are the remains of old meanders which have been cut off from the main river during a flood.

During flood conditions the river has enormous energy and is able to break through the neck of land between two meanders. The river then takes the shortest route, quickly eroding a new channel. The river slowly deposits material, cutting off the old meander. In time the ox-bow lake becomes a marsh and eventually dries up.

Fig. 3.8 Ox-bow lake formation.

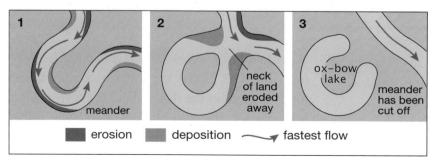

Flood plains

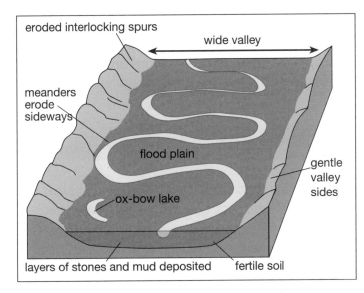

A flood plain is the flat valley floor found on either side of a river. Flood plains are formed by both erosion and deposition. The river erodes sideways as it meanders downstream, carving out a wide valley. The valley is also flooded each year when the river bursts its banks. During the flood the river deposits layers of stones and mud. The deposited material builds up in layers forming a flat valley floor.

Fig. 3.9 Flood plain.

Deltas

A delta is a low-lying area of land formed at a river's mouth. When a river reaches the sea it deposits its load. The heaviest material is deposited first, and the lightest last. If the sea is shallow, and does not have strong tides, the deposited material builds up to form a delta. Often the main river splits into many smaller rivers called **distributaries**.

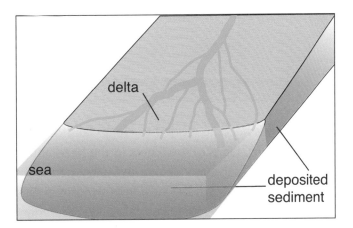

Fig. 3.10 River delta.

Progress Check

Cross out the incorrect words in the sentences below.

1 The upper course of a river contains a <u>V-shaped/U-shaped</u> valley.
2 The amount of water in a river <u>increases/decreases</u> towards the mouth.
3 The place where a river begins is called the <u>mouth/source</u>.
4   A curve in a river is called a <u>meander/ox-bow lake</u>.
5 The flat valley floor next to a river is known as a <u>delta/flood plain</u>.

Incorrect words: 1. U-shaped. 2. Decreases. 3. Mouth. 4. Ox-bow lake. 5. Delta.

3.5 Coastal landscapes

Key Point

Coastlines are dynamic areas where landforms are constantly being created and destroyed by the power of waves.

Headlands and bays

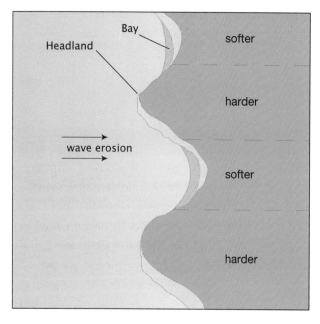

Headlands and bays are usually found in areas with different rock types. The softer rocks are eroded more quickly by waves, forming bays. The harder rocks are left behind to form headlands with steep cliffs sticking out to sea.

Bays also form where there are areas of weakness (faults) running through rock.

Fig. 3.11 Headlands and bays.

Caves, arches, stacks and stumps

Headlands become eroded to create landforms called caves, arches, stacks and stumps. Lines of weakness in the headland, called faults, are attacked by waves. Over many years the faults open up into **caves**. Eventually some caves break through the headland to form **arches**. The arches then collapse, leaving large pillars called **stacks**. When a stack falls over, its rocky base remains as a **stump**.

Fig. 3.12 Caves, arches, stacks and stumps.

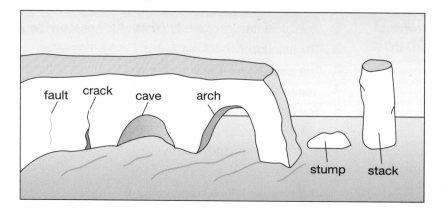

Beaches

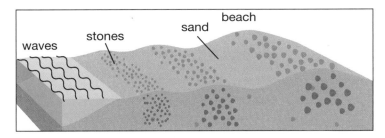

beach
sand
stones
waves

Fig. 3.13 Beach.

A beach is a deposit of sand and stones along a coast. Beaches are formed by the transportation and deposition of material by waves.

> The ridges along a beach are called berms.

Sources of beach material:
- Cliffs which are eroded by waves.
- Material deposited at the coast by rivers.
- Material transported from further along the coast.
- Offshore shingle banks.

Longshore drift

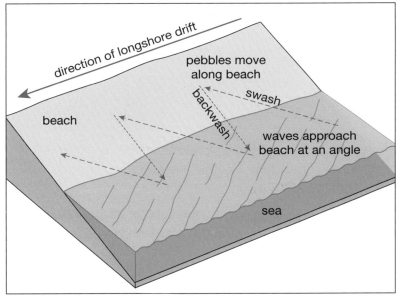

direction of longshore drift

pebbles move along beach

swash

backwash

beach

waves approach beach at an angle

sea

Fig. 3.14 Longshore drift.

The movement of beach material along the coast by waves is called **longshore drift**.
- Waves approach the beach at the angle of the prevailing wind.
- Swash carries material up the beach at an angle.
- Backwash drags material straight down the beach.
- Material is moved along the shore in a zig-zag pattern.

Swash is the movement of a wave up a beach, and backwash is the movement of a wave back down a beach.

Spits

A spit is a curved beach which extends into the sea at a river mouth, or where there is a break in the coastline. Longshore drift moves beach material along the coast. Where the coastline changes direction, and longshore drift continues, a spit may develop.

As a spit grows it will develop a 'hooked end' if the wind sometimes blows from the other direction. In the middle of the spit, sand dunes develop from wind-blown sand. In the sheltered area behind the spit, mud is deposited and a salt-marsh develops.

> Salt marshes provide a habitat for several rare plants and animals.

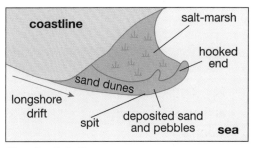

coastline

salt-marsh

hooked end

sand dunes

longshore drift

spit

deposited sand and pebbles

sea

Fig. 3.15 Spit.

Progress Check

1 Label the features marked a) to e) on the diagram below.

1. (a) = fault, (b) = cave, (c) = arch, (d) = stump, (e) = stack.

3.6 Hazards

Key Point

A mega-tsunami is a hazard caused by a landslide, resulting in massive coastal flooding.

Something which poses a risk to people, property and the environment is known as a hazard. Hazards include volcanic eruptions, earthquakes, landslides and floods.

In recent years scientists have discovered a new type of hazard called a mega-tsunami. A mega-tsunami is a giant sea wave which causes devastation to coastal areas.

Causes

Tsunamis caused by earthquakes have a maximum height of about 40 metres.

Mega-tsunamis are caused by landslides into the sea. Thankfully they are very rare, with only 11 occurring during the past 200 000 years. The most recent mega-tsunami happened in a remote area of Alaska in 1958.

The next mega-tsunami is likely to be caused by the collapse of a volcano called Cumbre Vieja, on the island of La Palma. Scientists predict that at some point in the future the volcano will erupt, and a landslide weighing 500 thousand million tonnes will crash into the sea. This will result in a wave 650 metres high speeding across the Atlantic Ocean at 500 mph.

Effects

Morocco would be the first area to be hit by 100-metre-high waves. Six hours later Spain, Portugal, France and the UK would be hit by waves

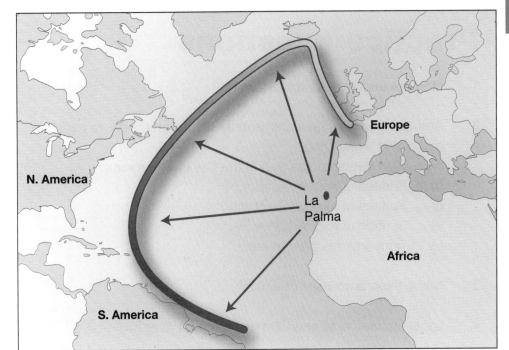

Fig. 3.16
Approximate mega-tsunami track after 6 hours.

12 metres high. The densely populated coastlines of North and South America would be hit by a 50-metre-high wall of water nine hours after the landslide. The wave would travel up to 12 miles inland, destroying everything in its path.

Human response

There is nothing that people can do to stop a mega-tsunami. However, scientists are monitoring Cumbre Vieja carefully for any signs of eruption. If an eruption was predicted, huge areas of coastline would have to be evacuated. Luckily, the volcano may not erupt for hundreds, or even thousands, of years.

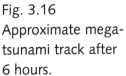

Progress Check

True or false?
1 Mega-tsunamis are caused by earthquakes.
2 The most recent mega-tsunami happened in Alaska.
3 A mega-tsunami can be over 500 metres high.
4 Mega-tsunamis can travel at 500 mph.
5 The UK could not be affected by a mega-tsunami.

1. False. 2. True. 3. True. 4. True. 5. False.

Practice questions

1   How are sedimentary rocks formed?   **(2)**

2   Arrange the following statements in the correct order to explain
     onion-skin weathering.   **(5)**
   a)   High temperatures during the day heat the rock.
   b)   Surface of rock peels away.
   c)   Surface of rock contracts.
   d)   Surface of rock expands.
   e)   Temperatures drop at night.

3   Name three processes of erosion.   **(3)**

4   Label features a) to e) on the diagram of a river basin below.   **(5)**

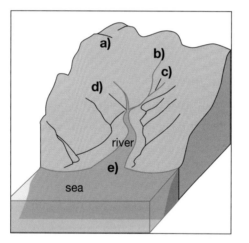

5   Draw a diagram to explain the process of longshore drift.   **(4)**

4 Weather and climate

The topics covered in this chapter are:

- The water cycle
- Weather
- Rain
- Anticyclones and depressions
- Climate
- Britain's climate
- Microclimates

After studying this topic you should be able to:

- understand how the water cycle works
- describe the different types of weather
- explain what causes rain
- understand the weather caused by anticyclones and depressions
- understand why climates differ
- describe and explain Britain's climate
- understand rural and urban microclimates.

4.1 The water cycle

The water on the Earth today is the same water that was here when dinosaurs roamed the planet.

Key Point	The water cycle is the continuous circling of water between the sea, atmosphere and land.

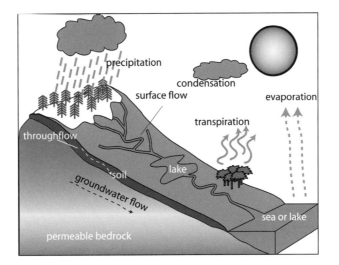

Fig. 4.1
The water cycle.

- **Evaporation** – water in the sea and lakes is heated by the sun. It evaporates, becomes water vapour and rises into the atmosphere.
- **Transpiration** – water vapour is released from the leaves of trees and plants. It rises into the atmosphere.
- **Condensation** – air cools as it rises and water vapour condenses to form clouds of tiny water droplets.
- **Precipitation** – water droplets collide and form raindrops. When they become heavy enough they fall to Earth as rain.
- **Surface flow** – water flows in rivers back to the sea.
- **Through flow** – water flows slowly through soil towards the sea.
- **Groundwater flow** – water flows very slowly through porous rock towards the sea.

> 80 per cent of precipitation falls directly into the sea.

People and the water cycle

Fresh water is a vital resource needed for people to survive. People interrupt the water cycle to obtain water for homes, farming and industry in a number of ways.

- **Dams** are built across rivers to form large lakes called **reservoirs**.
- **Boreholes** are drilled into the ground and fresh water is pumped up from the porous rocks below.
- **Cloud-seeding** is a technique which is used mainly in the USA. Rockets are fired into the air, which explode into thousands of tiny pieces. The tiny pieces cause water droplets to form, creating clouds.
- **Desalination plants** remove salt from seawater so it can be used by people. This technique is used in several hot and dry countries such as Malta and Libya.

Progress Check

1 What is the water cycle?

2 Match the descriptions below to the key words.

a) Trees and plants release water vapour from tiny holes in their leaves.

b) Temperatures decrease with height, causing water vapour to form clouds.

c) Water droplets collide and form raindrops.

d) Water in the sea is heated by the sun and becomes water vapour.

evaporation   transpiration   condensation   precipitation

1. The continuous circling of water between the sea, atmosphere and land. 2. (a) = transpiration, (b) = condensation, (c) = precipitation, (d) = evaporation.

4.2 Weather

What is weather?

> **Key Point**
>
> Weather is the condition of the atmosphere at a certain place and time.

Types of weather

Temperature:
- Describes how hot or cold the air is.
- Measured with a thermometer.
- Recorded in degrees Celsius (°C).

Precipitation:
- Deposition of water from the atmosphere.
- Precipitation includes rain, hail, sleet, snow and fog.
- Measured with a rain gauge.
- Recorded in millimetres (mm).

Air pressure:
- The weight of the atmosphere.
- Warm air rising = low pressure.
- Cool air sinking = high pressure.
- Measured with a barometer.
- Recorded in millibars (mb).

Wind:
- The horizontal movement of air.
- Wind blows from areas of high pressure to areas of low pressure.
- Wind direction is measured with a wind vane.
- Wind speed is measured with an anemometer (knots, km/per hour and Beaufort Scale).

> Wind direction is described by the direction wind is blowing *from*.

Clouds:
- Water droplets or ice crystals held in the atmosphere.
- Measured by observation.
- Recorded in eighths of sky (oktas) covered by clouds.

> All weather is powered by energy from the sun.

Fig. 4.2 An anemometer.

Weather forecasting

Weather has a huge impact on people's lives.

Things affected by weather:
- farming
- sport
- transport
- energy use
- work
- tourism.

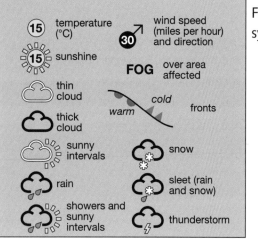

Fig. 4.3 Weather symbols.

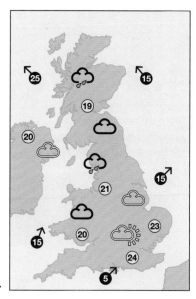

Fig. 4.4 Weather map.

It is therefore very important to try to predict what the weather will be like. Weather data is collected by weather stations, ships, aircraft and satellites. The data is processed using computers and analysed by weather experts, called meteorologists. Meteorologists use the data to forecast what the weather will be like for the next three or four days. This allows people to plan ahead – for example, by gritting the roads if temperatures are going to drop below freezing.

Weather forecasts are available on the radio, television, Internet and in newspapers. Weather symbols on a map are generally used to show what the weather will be like.

Progress Check

1 What is weather?

2 Match the types of weather below with the instruments used to measure them.

a) Temperature

b) Precipitation

c) Air pressure

d) Wind speed

anemometer   thermometer   rain gauge   barometer

1. The condition of the atmosphere at a certain place and time. 2. (a) = thermometer, (b) = rain gauge, (c) = barometer, (d) = anemometer.

4.3 Rain

Key Point

There are three different types of rainfall.

Snow is formed in a similar way to rain, except that water vapour freezes into crystals of ice.

Rain results when air containing water vapour is forced to rise. As air rises higher into the atmosphere it cools down. Water vapour condenses to form clouds of tiny water droplets. The water droplets collide and grow to form raindrops. When the raindrops are heavy enough they fall as rain.

Relief rainfall

The west of the UK receives relief rainfall. This is a result of moist Atlantic winds being forced to rise as they reach high land on the coast.

Relief rainfall happens when moist air is forced to rise over hills and mountains. As the air rises, water vapour cools and condenses to form clouds. The clouds release rainfall over the hills and mountains. When the air has passed over the high land it descends and the process is reversed. The air warms up and remaining clouds are evaporated.

The sheltered side of a hill or mountain is known as the 'rain shadow' because very little rain falls there.

Frontal rainfall

Much of the rainfall in Britain is caused by fronts, as moist, warm Atlantic air collides with cool air from northern Europe.

Frontal rainfall results when a moist, warm air mass collides with a cool air mass. The two air masses will not mix because they are different temperatures. As a result, the cool air undercuts the warm air, forcing the warm air mass to rise. As the warm air rises, it cools, water vapour condenses, and it rains. The boundary between the two air masses is called a **front**. It is along the fronts that most rainfall occurs.

Convectional rainfall

Convectional rainfall occurs only on hot summer days in the UK.

Convectional rainfall happens on hot days. The sun heats the Earth's surface, evaporating large amounts of water. Water vapour is lifted high into the atmosphere in the rising warm air. As the air rises it cools and the water vapour condenses to form huge anvil-shaped storm clouds (cumulonimbus). Heavy rainfall occurs, often accompanied by thunder and lightning. Convectional rainfall happens daily in equatorial regions.

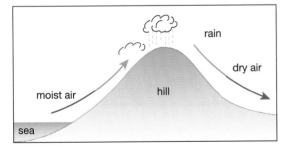

Fig. 4.5 Relief rainfall.

Fig. 4.6 Frontal rainfall.

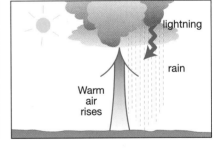

Fig. 4.7 Convectional rainfall.

Progress Check

1 Arrange the following statements in the correct order to explain how relief rainfall happens.

   a) Water vapour condenses to form clouds.

   b) High land forces moist air to rise.

   c) Clouds evaporate as the air descends.

   d) Moist air cools as it goes higher.

   e) Rainfall occurs over the hills.

1. (b), (d), (a), (e), (c).

4.4 Anticyclones and depressions

Key Point

Anticyclones bring dry weather, depressions result in wet weather.

Anticyclones

An anticyclone is the weather caused by a cool, dry air mass.

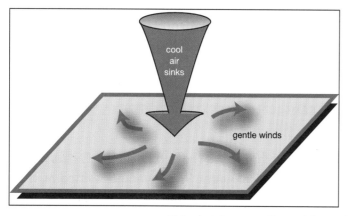

Fig. 4.8 Anticyclone.

Anticyclones only rarely affect the British Isles. Occasionally, dry air masses from Europe or North Africa move over Britain. Anticyclones are slow-moving, which means we may have dry, bright and settled weather for several days, or even weeks.

Winds blow gently out from the centre of high pressure. In the northern hemisphere the winds blow clockwise, and in the southern hemisphere, anticlockwise. This is due to the rotation of the Earth.

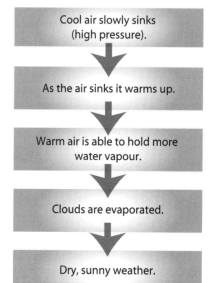

Cool air slowly sinks (high pressure).

As the air sinks it warms up.

Warm air is able to hold more water vapour.

Clouds are evaporated.

Dry, sunny weather.

Summer anticyclone	Winter anticyclone
Sunny	Sunny
Light winds	Light winds
High temperatures	Low temperatures
Good visibility	Ice and fog

Depressions

An occluded front is formed if the warm air mass is completely undercut by the cool air mass.

A depression is an area of low pressure, formed when a warm, moist air mass and a cool, dry air mass meet.

Warm air rises at the centre of a depression. This causes low air pressure and air is drawn in from the sides, forming strong winds. In the northern

Fig. 4.9 A depression.

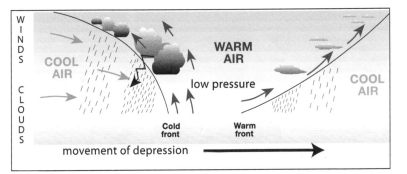

Air masses of different temperatures will not mix.
↓
Warm air rises over cool air to form a warm front.
↓
Cool air undercuts warm air from behind to form a cold front.
↓
Warm air is forced to rise along both fronts.
↓
Water vapour cools, condenses, clouds form and it rains.

> The lower the air pressure, the stronger the winds.

hemisphere the winds blow anticlockwise, and in the southern hemisphere, clockwise.

The British Isles are greatly affected by depressions. Moist, warm air blowing across the Atlantic Ocean collides with cool dry air blowing across Europe. Large depressions are formed, which take two or three days to pass over. This means Britain has clouds, strong winds and rain for much of the year.

Progress Check

1 Complete the following sentences using the words below.

a) A depression is an area of _____ pressure.

b) Low air pressure results in _____ winds.

c) Warm air is undercut from behind to form a _____ front.

d) A depression is formed when a _____ air mass meets a cool air mass.

e) An occluded front is formed when warm air is lifted off the ground by _____ air.

low   cold   warm   cool   fast

1. (a) = low, (b) = fast, (c) = cold, (d) = warm, (e) = cool.

4.5 Climate

Key Point

Climate is the average weather conditions of a place, based on data recorded over 40 years.

Global climates

> Climate statistics give only monthly averages, and hide any day-to-day variations.

The world can be classified into different climate zones which have similar patterns of temperature and precipitation.

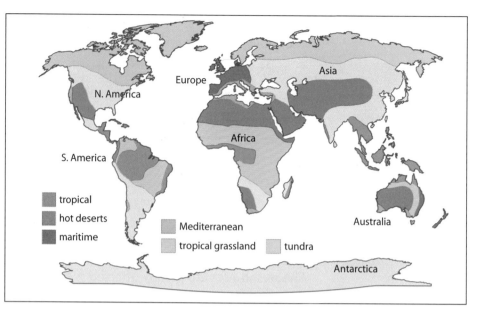

Fig. 4.10. World climate regions.

Tropical:
- Hot all year.
- Heavy rain all year.

Desert:
- Hot all year.
- Very little rain.

Maritime:
- Moderate temperatures all year.
- Rain all year.

Mediterranean:
- Hot dry summers.
- Mild wet winters.

Tropical grassland:
- Hot all year.
- Wet and dry seasons.

Tundra:
- Short cool summer.
- Long cold winter.

Factors affecting climate

There are five key factors that affect the climate of an area.

Latitude

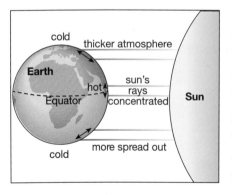

Latitude describes how far north or south a place is from the equator. The sun's energy is concentrated at the equator. This results in high temperatures all year, and daily convectional rainfall.

The strength of the sun's rays decreases with distance north or south from the equator. This is because they are spread over a wider area, and have to pass through a thicker band of atmosphere. This means temperatures fall towards the North and South Poles.

Fig. 4.11 The effect of latitude.

Altitude

Altitude is the height above sea level. The higher a place, the colder it is. This is because light from the sun is absorbed and re-radiated as heat by the Earth's surface. This heat warms the lower layer of the atmosphere, which means that temperatures drop by approximately 6.5°C with every 1000 metres of altitude. Higher areas also receive more precipitation because of relief rainfall.

Distance from the sea

Coastal areas also receive more precipitation due to moist air being blown inland.

Distance from the sea affects temperature and precipitation. Areas close to the sea have a maritime climate. The sea keeps coastal areas warmer in winter, and cooler in summer. This means that they have a small annual temperature range.

Inland areas tend to be drier than coastal areas.

Inland areas, which are not influenced by the sea, have a continental climate. It can be very hot in summer, and very cold in winter. They have a large annual temperature range.

Ocean currents

Ocean currents are large flows of warm or cold water in the sea.
- Warm currents flow from the tropics towards the North and South Poles. These currents warm coastal areas in winter, but also bring rain.
- Cold ocean currents flow from the poles towards the equator. These currents lower temperatures in coastal areas.

Prevailing winds

Prevailing winds are the winds that blow most frequently. Winds can affect temperature and precipitation.
- Winds blowing from tropical areas bring warm weather, while winds blowing from polar areas bring cold weather.
- Winds blowing over oceans cause precipitation, while winds that have blown over land are dry.

Progress Check

1 Match the descriptions below with the correct climate type.
a) Very hot and dry all year.
b) Hot all year and rains every day.
c) Cool in summer and very cold in winter.
d) Hot all year with a wet season and a dry season.
e) Hot in summer and mild in winter.

Mediterranean   desert   tropical grassland   tropical   tundra

1. (a) = desert, (b) = tropical, (c) = tundra, (d) = tropical grassland, (e) = Mediterranean.

4.6 Britain's climate

> **Key Point**
>
> Britain has a temperate maritime climate. This means that the climate is moderate and is influenced by the sea.

Britain's weather is dominated by frontal depressions which blow in from the Atlantic, bringing wind and rain. Occasionally, anticyclones move over Britain from Europe or North Africa. This results in settled dry weather, which is cold in winter but warm in summer.

Summer temperatures

During the summer the warmest places in Britain are in the south, with average temperatures of 17°C. Temperatures decrease towards the north, to an average of 13°C in Scotland. The reason for this is that temperatures fall with distance from the equator.

Winter temperatures

During the winter the warmest places in Britain are on the south-west coast, with average temperatures of 7°C. This can be explained by the North Atlantic Drift, a warm ocean current which flows across the Atlantic from the Gulf of Mexico. Temperatures decrease towards the north-east, to an average of 4°C.

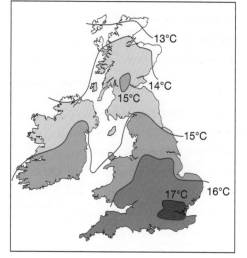

Fig. 4.12 Summer temperatures in the UK.

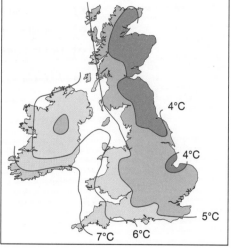

Fig. 4.13 Winter temperatures in the UK.

Precipitation

It rains regularly throughout the year in Britain, but not all areas receive the same amount.

- The wettest areas are the west coast of Scotland and the Welsh mountains. These areas can receive over 2000 mm of precipitation per year. This is relief rainfall caused by the high land.
- The driest areas are in the south-east, where some places receive only 600 mm of precipitation per year. This is because the east of the country is in the rain shadow.

West Scotland receives as much rainfall as an average rainforest!

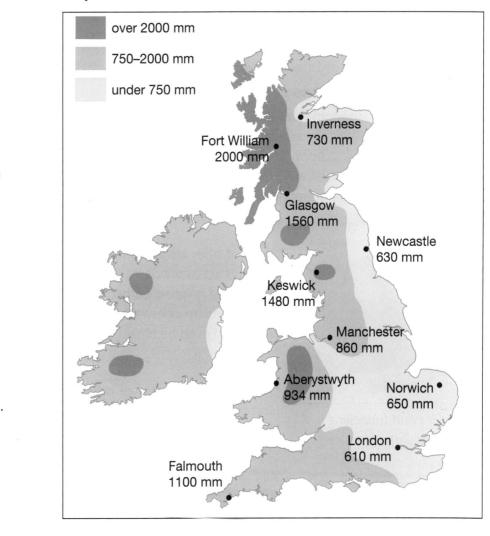

over 2000 mm

750–2000 mm

under 750 mm

Inverness 730 mm

Fort William 2000 mm

Glasgow 1560 mm

Newcastle 630 mm

Keswick 1480 mm

Manchester 860 mm

Aberystwyth 934 mm

Norwich 650 mm

London 610 mm

Falmouth 1100 mm

Fig. 4.14 Annual precipitation in the UK.

Progress Check

1 What type of climate does Britain have?
2 Which area is warmest during the summer?
3 Which area is warmest during the winter?
4 What is the name of the warm ocean current which flows up the west coast of Britain?
5 Where are the wettest areas in Britain?

1. Temperate maritime. 2. South. 3. South-west. 4. North Atlantic Drift.
5. West coast of Scotland and Wales.

4.7 Microclimates

What is a microclimate?

Key Point — A microclimate is the climate of a relatively small area such as a city or a farm.

City microclimates

Temperature

In cities during the day, buildings and dark tarmac roads absorb heat from the sun and store it. At night the heat is slowly released. Heat also escapes from cars, central heating and power stations. All this heat warms up cities so that at night they can be 4 or 5°C warmer than the surrounding countryside.

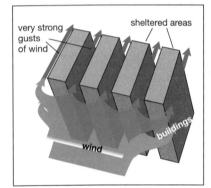

Fig. 4.15 Wind funnelling around buildings.

Wind

Winds in cities are generally not as fast as in the countryside. Tall buildings act as windbreaks, slowing the wind. However, in some places wind is funnelled between the buildings creating extremely strong gusts. In cities with many skyscrapers, such as New York, people can even be blown over.

Rain

Cities receive up to 30 per cent more rainfall than the countryside. Heat rising from the city causes thunderstorms and convectional rainfall. However, because cities are warmer, they receive less snow than the countryside.

Countryside

Temperature

The shape of the land (relief) in the countryside affects temperatures.

In the northern hemisphere:

- South-facing slopes are warm because they face the sun. They are best suited for growing crops.
- North-facing slopes are cold because they are in shade, and are more exposed to cold northerly winds. They are best used for sheep farming.

Wind

Winds can be very strong in open countryside, especially in upland areas. Farmers often plant hedges and build walls along the sides of their fields to act as windbreaks. Animals are given protection from cold winds and crops are less likely to be blown over.

Rain

Although on average the countryside receives less rainfall than cities, upland areas may suffer from heavy rainfall, fog and snow.

Progress Check

True or false?

1 Cities are warmer than the countryside at night.

2 Cities are windier than the countryside.

3 Cities receive more snow than the countryside.

4 Cities receive more rain than the countryside.

5 In the northern hemisphere, north-facing slopes are the sunniest.

1. True. 2. False. 3. False. 4. True. 5. False.

Practice questions

1 Match the types of weather with the correct unit of measurement. **(5)**

Temperature   Millimetres
Precipitation   Millibars
Air pressure   Degrees Celsius
Wind speed   Oktas
Cloud cover   Kilometres per hour

2 Name the three types of rainfall shown in the diagrams below. **(3)**

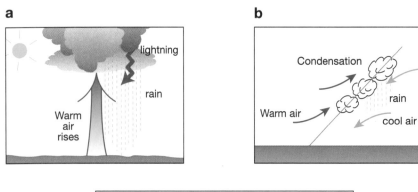

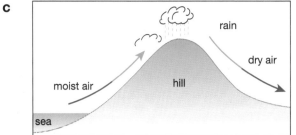

3 Describe the type of weather caused by an anticyclone in the summer. **(2)**

4 Describe the type of weather caused by a depression in the winter. **(2)**

5 Underline the correct words to show the impacts of an urban microclimate. **(3)**

Impacts of urban microclimate

Average temperature	Hotter	Colder
Average rainfall	Wetter	Drier
Average windspeed	Faster	Slower

5 Ecosystems

The topics covered in this chapter are:

- Ecosystems, energy and nutrients
- Deciduous woodlands
- Desert ecosystems
- Tropical grassland ecosystems
- Tropical rainforests

After studying this topic you should be able to:

- explain what ecosystems are and where they are located
- explain how energy and nutrients are transferred in ecosystems
- describe deciduous woodland ecosystems
- describe desert ecosystems
- describe tropical grassland ecosystems
- describe tropical rainforest ecosystems.

5.1 Ecosystems

What is an ecosystem?

Key Point

An ecosystem is a community of trees, plants, animals and insects living in a particular environment.

- The living things in an ecosystem are closely linked together, and depend on the land, water and air for their survival.
- Ecosystems range in size from a small pond to a huge area of forest, which stretches across a continent.
- The Earth may be thought of as one giant ecosystem.

Global distribution of ecosystems

Over thousands of years, trees, plants, animals and insects have adapted to different conditions around the world.

Variations in sunlight, temperature and rainfall have resulted in the evolution of eight major different types of ecosystem. Each ecosystem has distinctive characteristics.

- **Tundra** – short plants, such as moss, heather and lichen; some stunted trees.
- **Coniferous forest** – dense evergreen trees, such as fir and pine; few other species.
- **Deciduous forest** – trees that shed their leaves in winter, such as oak and ash; shrubs and short grasses.
- **Temperate grassland** – grasses up to 2 metres tall; some trees, such as willow.

Notice how the map shows that the same ecosystems are found on similar lines of latitude.

The ecosystem map can be misleading, because in many places the natural ecosystem has been destroyed to make room for farmland and buildings.

Fig. 5.1 Global distribution of ecosystems.

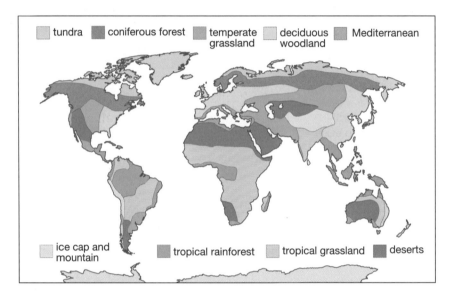

| tundra | coniferous forest | temperate grassland | deciduous woodland | Mediterranean |
| ice cap and mountain | | tropical rainforest | tropical grassland | deserts |

- **Mediterranean** – evergreen woodland, such as cork and pine; thorny shrubs with thin waxy leaves.
- **Desert** – drought resistant plants, such as cacti, with very long roots to reach deep water supplies.
- **Tropical grassland** – drought resistant trees with waxy leaves and thorns; grasses up to 5 metres tall.
- **Tropical rainforest** – hundreds of different species of tree; some trees are over 50 metres tall.

Progress Check

1 What is an ecosystem?
2 Match the descriptions below with the correct ecosystems.
   a) Dense evergreen trees with few other species.
   b) Drought resistant trees with waxy leaves.
   c) Cacti with long roots to reach water.
   d) Oak and ash trees which lose their leaves in winter.
   e) Stunted trees, moss, heather and lichen.

   tropical grassland   desert   coniferous forest

   tundra   deciduous woodland

1. A community of trees, plants, animals and insects living in a particular environment. 2. (a) coniferous forest, (b) tropical grassland, (c) desert, (d) deciduous woodland, (e) tundra.

5.2 Energy and nutrients

Food chains

> **Key Point**
>
> All living things need energy to survive. Energy flows through an ecosystem along a food chain.

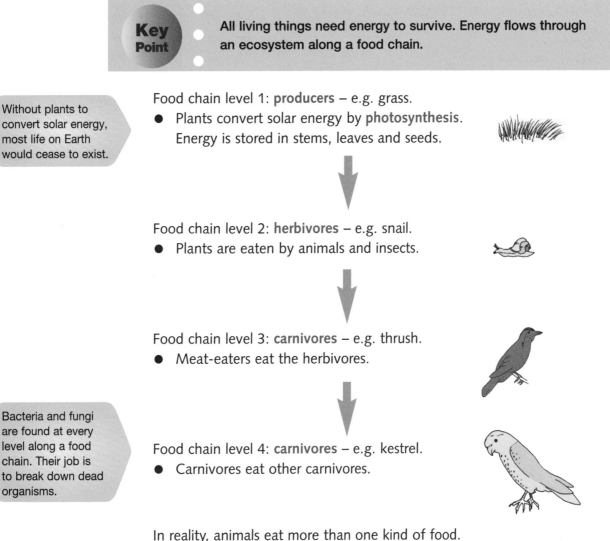

Without plants to convert solar energy, most life on Earth would cease to exist.

Food chain level 1: **producers** – e.g. grass.
● Plants convert solar energy by **photosynthesis**. Energy is stored in stems, leaves and seeds.

Food chain level 2: **herbivores** – e.g. snail.
● Plants are eaten by animals and insects.

Food chain level 3: **carnivores** – e.g. thrush.
● Meat-eaters eat the herbivores.

Bacteria and fungi are found at every level along a food chain. Their job is to break down dead organisms.

Food chain level 4: **carnivores** – e.g. kestrel.
● Carnivores eat other carnivores.

In reality, animals eat more than one kind of food.
This means food chains become inter-connected to create food webs.

Nutrient cycles

> **Key Point**
>
> Plants and animals also need nutrients to survive. Nutrients are chemicals that are used by living things to grow.

Nutrients are released from rock as it is weathered underground. Trees and plants absorb nutrients through their roots. Animals get nutrients either by eating the plants, or by eating other animals.

When the plants and animals die, their remains are broken down by bacteria and fungi. This allows the nutrients to be washed back into the soil. The nutrient cycle then begins again.

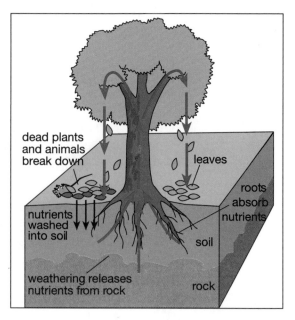

Fig. 5.2 The nutrient cycle.

How do people modify ecosystems?

People may interfere with energy flows and nutrient cycles in ecosystems – not always deliberately.

● The **introduction** or **extinction** of a **species** of plant or animal will alter the balance of food webs. Example: introduction of cane toads to Australia in 1935 in an attempt to control the sugar cane beetle.

● Farmers **add nutrients** to ecosystems in the form of **fertilisers**, but then remove nutrients when the crops are harvested.

Progress Check

1 Arrange the following statements in the correct order to explain how the nutrient cycle works.

a) Dead plants and animals are broken down by bacteria.

b) Rainwater washes nutrients back into the soil.

c) Bedrock is broken down by weathering and releases nutrients into the soil.

d) The roots of trees and plants absorb nutrients from the soil.

e) Carnivores eat herbivores.

f) Herbivores eat the leaves of trees and plants.

1. (c), (d), (f), (e), (a), (b).

5.3 Deciduous woodlands

Location

● Deciduous woodlands are located between 40 and 60° north and south of the equator.

● Deciduous woodlands grow in Europe, eastern North America, northern China, Japan and New Zealand.

Climate

Deciduous woodlands have four seasons during the year: spring, summer, autumn and winter.

- Temperatures are mild in winter, averaging 4°C. Summers are warm, with an average of 16°C.
- Frontal rainfall occurs throughout the year. Some places can receive over 2000 mm of rainfall per year.

Soil

Deciduous woodlands have a brown soil. Brown soils can be quite deep and are fertile. Nutrients in the soil are recycled quickly because there are lots of insects to help break down any decaying matter.

Vegetation

The vegetation in deciduous woodlands can be divided into four layers.
- **Tree layer** – broad-leaf trees such as oak, ash, chestnut, beech and elm.
- **Shrub layer** – hazel, holly and hawthorn.
- **Plant layer** – grasses, brambles, bracken and flowering plants, e.g. bluebells.
- **Floor layer** – fungi, moss and lichen.

Fig. 5.3 Deciduous woodland.

Wildlife

Deciduous woodlands contain large numbers of animals, birds and insects.
- Herbivores include worms, beetles, mice, shrews, rabbits, squirrels and deer.
- Carnivores include foxes, weasels, badgers, owls and hawks.

Human activity

There is almost no natural deciduous woodland left in Europe. Most woodland has been cleared to provide land for farming and to build settlements. The woodlands that remain have been modified by people. In the past deciduous trees were coppiced. This means they were cut down to ground level. The trees then re-grew as a number of stems. The stems were cut and used to make fences and furniture.

5.4 Desert ecosystems

Location

- Deserts are located between 15° and 30° north and south of the equator.
- The largest hot desert in the world is the Sahara, in north Africa. Other deserts around the world include the Kalahari (southern Africa), the Atacama (South America), the Gobi (Asia) and the Australian Desert.

Climate

- Very high temperatures throughout the year. Average daytime temperature 30°C, with extremes of over 50°C. Temperatures can fall to 0°C at night.
- Very little rainfall due to constant high air pressure. On average, deserts receive less than 250mm of rainfall each year.

Soils

Desert soils are grey in colour. They are thin and have little organic matter. Because water is evaporated so quickly, salt builds up on the surface of the soil. Desert soils are not very fertile.

Vegetation

Climate adaptations:
- Cacti store water in fleshy stems.
- Plants have thick, waxy skins to reduce water loss.
- Cacti have spikes to prevent animals eating them.
- Plant roots grow deep or wide to soak up as much water as possible.
- Trees have thick bark to protect against fire.

Fig. 5.4 Desert cacti.

Wildlife

Desert ecosystems have simple food webs, and are therefore very fragile environments.

Deserts can support a surprising amount of wildlife. Desert animals include termites, spiders, lizards, snakes, kangaroos, dingoes and camels.

Human activity

People have lived in deserts for thousands of years. For example, Australian aborigines survived by hunting animals and gathering fruit, nuts and plants. Their deep knowledge of the desert ecosystem meant they did not damage it. However, modern farming practices have altered the edges of desert ecosystems. Overgrazing by goats and sheep has caused soil erosion, and irrigation has made the soil salty. As a result deserts are growing larger.

Progress Check

True or false?
1 Deserts are located on the equator.
2 The largest desert in the world is the Kalahari.
3 Deserts can reach temperatures of over 50°C.
4 Desert soils are very fertile.
5 Some desert trees are fire-proof.

1. False. 2. False. 3. True. 4. False. 5. True.

5.5 Tropical grassland ecosystems

Location

- Tropical grasslands are located between 5° and 15° north and south of the equator.
- Tropical grasslands are found in South America, Australia and Africa.

Climate

> Tropical grasslands have a wet season and a dry season. During the wet season the sun is overhead.

- Temperatures are high all year, with a monthly average of 25°C.
- Convectional rainfall occurs during the wet season. On average, tropical grasslands receive 1000 mm of precipitation each year.

Soil

The soil in tropical grasslands is a red clay. A hard layer of minerals forms just under the surface of the soil. This makes it difficult to plough and farm. The soil is not very fertile.

Vegetation

Tropical grassland is a zone of transition between tropical rainforest and desert.

Fig. 5.5 Acacia tree.

Climate adaptations:
- Acacia trees have developed long roots. The roots grow deep in the soil, but also spread outwards, to absorb as much water as possible. Acacia trees also have waxy leaves, which they lose during the dry season to conserve water.
- Grasses grow quickly to make the most of the rainy season. They reach a height of between three and five metres. Although the grasses die back during the dry season, their seeds lie dormant on the surface, waiting for next year's rain.

Wildlife

Tropical grasslands can support many species of animals, and have a complex food web.

● Herbivores include elephants, zebra, wildebeest, rhinos, giraffe and antelope.

● Carnivores include lions, cheetahs and hyenas.

Human activity

Crops such as millet, tobacco and maize can be grown in tropical grassland ecosystems. However, because the rain is unreliable, crops sometimes fail, resulting in famine.

Tropical grasslands are most suitable for grazing cattle or goats (pastoral farming). Traditionally, farmers moved around with their animals to find areas of fresh grassland. However, where overgrazing occurs the soil is easily blown or washed away. As a result, many areas of tropical grassland are becoming desert. This process is called **desertification**.

Progress Check

1 Cross out the incorrect words in the sentences below.

a) Tropical grasslands are located between 5 and 15/50 degrees north and south of the equator.

b) Tropical grasslands experience high/low temperatures all year.

c) Trees in tropical grasslands are coniferous/deciduous.

d) Tropical grassland soils are fertile/infertile.

e) Tropical grasslands are well suited to pastoral/arable farming.

Incorrect words: (a) 50, (b) low, (c) coniferous, (d) fertile, (e) arable.

5.6 Tropical rainforests

Location

Tropical rainforests contain 90 per cent of all known species of plants and animals.

- Tropical rainforests are located between 5° north and south of the equator.
- Tropical rainforests are found in South America, West Africa, South-east Asia and northern Australia.

Climate

Tropical rainforests are not as hot as deserts, because they are cloudy in the afternoon. However, because rainforests are so humid, they feel very hot and sticky.

- Temperatures are high throughout the year, with an average of 27°C.
- Humidity is high.
- Convectional rainfall occurs daily, and on average tropical rainforests receive over 2000 mm of precipitation each year.

Soils

Most of the nutrients in tropical rainforests are stored in the trees and plants.

The soil in a tropical rainforest is red clay. Rock is weathered quickly in hot, wet climates, so rainforest soils can be up to 20 metres deep. Although the soil is very deep, it is not fertile.

Fig. 5.6 Rainforest.

Vegetation

A hectare of Brazilian rainforest may contain 500 different species of tree and over 1000 different types of plant.

Rainforest vegetation can be divided into five layers. The tallest trees, called **emergents**, form the highest layer at 50 metres.

Climate adaptations:
- Trees grow tall so they can gain as much sunlight as possible.
- Trees have wide buttress roots to support their great height.
- Leaves are shiny and have pointed 'drip tips' to help shed heavy rainfall.
- Tree bark is thin because it never gets cold.

Wildlife

Rainforests contain thousands of species of insects, birds and animals. Most of the wildlife lives in the canopy layer, 30 metres above the forest floor.

There is a complex food web including creatures such as centipedes, spiders, beetles, frogs, squirrels, bats, parrots, monkeys and snakes. Many of these creatures live their whole lives in the tree-tops.

Human activity

Tropical rainforests are at risk of deforestation for the following reasons:
- **Agriculture** – forest is cleared to provide farmland.
- **Settlement** – land is needed to build homes.
- **Ranching** – forest is cleared to graze cattle.
- **Logging** – valuable timber is exported.
- **Mining** – minerals such as gold and iron ore are mined.
- **Dams** – rivers are dammed to provide hydro-electric power.

Progress Check

Complete the following sentences using the numbers below.

1 Tropical rainforests are located _____ degrees north and south of the equator.
2 The average precipitation in tropical rainforests is _____ millimetres per year.
3 The average temperature in tropical rainforests is _____ degrees Centigrade.
4 The red clay soils found in a tropical rainforest are up to _____ metres deep.
5 The tallest trees, emergents, can be over _____ metres tall.

5   27   2000   50   20

1. 5. 2. 2000. 3. 27. 4. 20. 5. 50.

Practice questions

1 Name ecosystems A–E on the map below. **(5)**

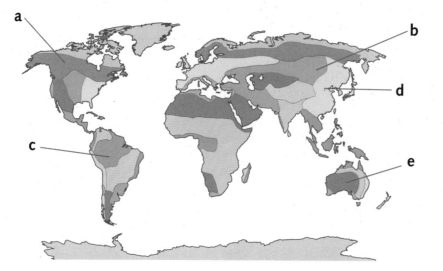

2 Arrange the following organisms into a food chain. **(5)**

killer whale   plankton   penguin   seal   shrimp

3 Match the type of vegetation with the correct ecosystem. **(4)**

Cactus	Deciduous woodland
Ash tree	Desert
Acacia tree	Tropical rainforest
Mahogany tree	Tropical grassland

4 Give three reasons to explain why tropical rainforests are being deforested. **(3)**

6 Population

The topics covered in this chapter are:

- Population density and distribution
- World population growth
- Differences in population growth
- Population control
- Migration and international migration

After studying this topic you should be able to:

- understand world population density and distribution
- understand the causes of global population growth
- account for differences in population growth between MEDCs and LEDCs
- understand population control
- identify different types of migration
- appreciate the causes and effects of international migration.

6.1 Population density and distribution

> **Key Point**
>
> Population means the number of people in a particular place.

Population density is the number of people per square kilometre.

Population distribution is how spread out a population is.

Try not to get confused between population density and population distribution.

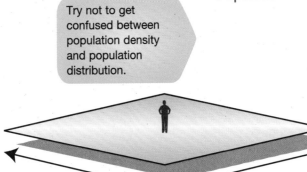

Fig. 6.1 Places with a low population density are said to be sparsely populated.

Fig. 6.2 Places with a high population density are said to be densely populated.

If you look at the map of the world you will see that the population is not evenly distributed. Some places are densely populated and some are sparsely populated.

> The map is a choropleth map (see topic 1.9). Choropleth maps show differences in densities by using shading or colours. The darker the shade or colour, the higher the density.

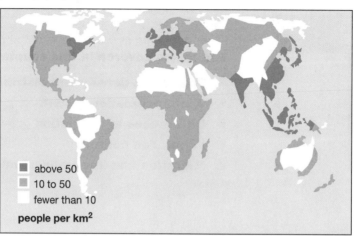

above 50
10 to 50
fewer than 10

people per km²

Fig. 6.3 World population density.

Parts of the world that are densely populated include Western Europe, South-east Asia, India and the east and west coasts of the USA.

Parts of the world that are sparsely populated include Canada, the west coast of South America, North Africa, Central Asia, North-eastern Europe and Central Australia.

Reasons for the differences in world population density are given in the table. Positive factors make it easier for people to live in a place, negative factors make it harder.

Factor	Positive	Negative
relief	flat land	mountainous land
climate	warm, enough rain	very hot, very cold, too dry
vegetation	open grassland	dense forest
soils	deep fertile soil	thin infertile soil
resources	coal, minerals and timber	few natural resources
access	coastal areas	inland areas
economy	plenty of industry and jobs	lack of industry and jobs

Progress Check

Complete the sentences using the words below.

1 Canada has a population density that is _____.

2 A map that shows differences in density is known as a _____ map.

3 Western Europe has a population density that is _____

choropleth   dense   sparse

1. sparse. 2. choropleth. 3. dense.

6.2 World population growth

Key Point The population of the world is not stable, it is growing at an increasing rate.

Population explosion

World population growth in the last 100 years has been so rapid that it has been described as a '**population explosion**'.

The graph shows that the world's population stayed at about 250 million people between 0 AD and 1000 AD. Since then, a population of 1 billion people was reached in 1820, 2 billion in 1960, 4 billion in 1974 and 6 billion in 1999.

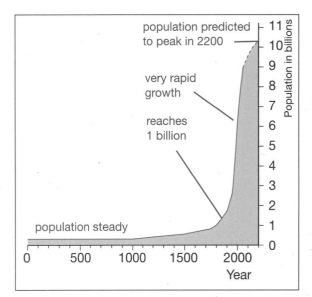

Fig. 6.4 World population growth.

Key Point The world's population is predicted to peak in 2200 at about 10.4 billion people and then stabilise.

Worldwide population growth is caused by **natural increase**. If more people are born than die, the population will increase.

Natural increase is the difference between the birth rate and the death rate. The **birth rate** is the number of babies born per thousand people a year. The **death rate** is the number of deaths per thousand people a year.

Why is the world's population growing so rapidly?

Fertility rate is sometimes used as an indicator of population growth. This is the average number of children born to each woman in a country.

The main reason for the population explosion is that the death rate has fallen dramatically over the last 100 years. This is due to improvements in healthcare, diet and sanitation (the hygienic disposal of human waste). If the death rate falls it means that people live longer so there are more people around. In addition, these people are more likely to live to adulthood and have children, so this creates even more people.

Progress Check

1 Why has the world's recent population growth been described as an explosion?
2 What is natural increase?
3 Why has the death rate fallen?

1. Because it has been so rapid. 2. The difference between the birth rate and death rate. 3. Because of improvements in healthcare, diet and sanitation.

6.3 Differences in population growth

Key Point

Population growth rates are not the same across the world.

In 1999 the population of Europe increased by 266 000 people. The population of India increased by this amount every 6 days.

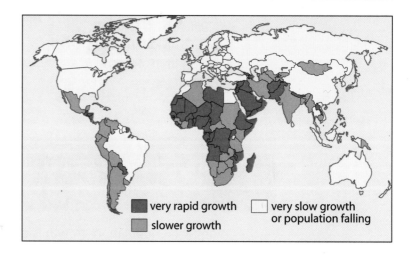

Fig. 6.5
Differences in world population growth.

Remember that birth rate, death rate and natural increase are the number per 1000 people.

On the map the UK is shown as having 'very slow growth or population falling'. The UK's birth rate is about 13 and the death rate is 11 – this means that every year there is a natural increase of only 2 people per thousand.

If you find Ghana on the world map you will see that it is a country experiencing 'very rapid growth'. Ghana's birth rate is about 34 and the death rate is 11, giving a natural increase of 22 people per thousand. In 1921 Ghana had just 2 million people; by 2000 the population had reached 20 million, a 1000 per cent rise in just 79 years.

Why does population grow so slowly in MEDCs?

An MEDC is a more economically developed country, e.g. the UK, the USA and Japan.

- More women are choosing to work, and delay getting married – this leaves less time for having children.
- Children are expensive. It costs about £100 000 to raise a child to his or her 18th birthday.
- People have a healthy diet and good health care, so most children survive to adulthood, meaning that parents limit the size of their families.
- Contraception is easily available.

Why does population grow so quickly in LEDCs?

An LEDC is a less economically developed country, e.g. Kenya, India and Brazil.

- Women marry at a young age, leaving more time in which to have children.
- Children are valuable because they can work.
- Children are needed to look after their parents in their old age.
- Women do not have the same rights as men. They cannot always choose whether to have children or not.
- In some areas, having many children improves a person's status.
- Many children die from illness. It is important to have several children to make sure some survive.
- Many people, especially women, are uneducated. They cannot choose a career instead of having children.
- Contraception is not always available.

Progress Check

1 Name the continent that has the most countries with very rapid population growth.
2 Describe the population growth in Australia.
3 Why do some women in MEDCs choose to have children later in life than women in LEDCs?

1. Africa. 2. Small growth or population falling. 3. Because they want to have a career first.

6.4 Population control

Rapid population growth in a country can cause problems. More hospitals, schools and jobs are required. Food has to be provided for the extra people and they need somewhere to live. For an LEDC this can put strain on an economy which is already stretched to the limit.

China's 'one child policy'

In 1979 China's population was fast approaching 1 billion people. If the growth did not slow down, the population would reach 1.8 billion by 2025. There would not be enough food to go round and millions would starve.

A number of strict rules were introduced:

- Couples need permission from the government to marry.
- Women must be at least 25 years old to marry.
- Couples need permission to have a child.
- Couples must agree to have only **one child**.

Couples with one child are given free health care, education, priority housing, a monthly allowance and an improved pension when they retire. Anyone who has more than one child has to pay back the benefits they received for their first child and pay a large fine.

How would you feel if the UK government said you were only allowed to have one child? What would it be like if you had no brothers or sisters, aunts, uncles or cousins?

Benefits

The policy has meant that 300 million potential new citizens were not born in the 1980s and 1990s. The average number of children born to a woman fell from 2.7 in 1979 to 1.9 in 1994. The population is expected to peak at 1.5 billion in 2050, before beginning to fall.

In the long term the quality of life for Chinese people should improve, as there will not be the catastrophic increase in population that was predicted.

The Chinese government helps couples by giving them advice about family planning. However, some women have been forced to have abortions or be sterilised.

Problems

- Elderly parents are left with no one to care for them if their child is a girl.
- There has been an increase in abortions of female foetuses, because couples want male babies.
- This means that the population will become unbalanced, with more men than women, and this could cause social problems in the future.
- Single children could become 'spoilt' because parents' attention is focused on their one child.

The tradition in China is that when women marry they go to live in the same place as their husband's family.

Progress Check

1 Why do some countries want to control their population growth?
2 How can countries control their population growth?
3 How big will China's population become before it begins to fall?

1. Because they cannot afford a larger population. 2. By promoting family planning or by passing laws.
3. 1.5 billion.

6.5 Migration

Migration is a movement of people from one place to another.

Any migration can be broken up into three parts:

Distance – how far someone has travelled.

Duration – how long the migration lasts for.

Decision – why the person migrated.

We can also divide migration into these types:

Internal migration is a move within a country, **international migration** is a move between countries.

Temporary migration is a move that lasts for less than a year, **permanent migration** is a move where the migrant expects to stay in their new location.

Voluntary migration is a move by choice, **forced migration** is a move against the migrant's will.

> **Key Point**
> Most decisions to migrate can be understood in terms of push and pull factors. A push factor is a reason why a person leaves their place of origin, a pull factor is a reason why a person is attracted to their destination.

Push factors	**Pull factors**
• not enough jobs	• higher standards of living
• natural disasters	• better-paid jobs
• wars	• better education
• drought	• family
• famine	• attractive environment

Migration in the UK

There are three main types of migration in the UK:

● **Commuting** – the daily migration between home and work.

● **Counterurbanisation** – the migration of people away from large cities to smaller towns or rural areas (this is also known as urban-rural migration).

● **North-south migration**: migration from the north of the UK to central and southern locations where there are more jobs and a better quality of life.

Progress Check

Classify each example of migration by completing the table.

1 Migration of Mexicans to the USA to find a better quality of life.
2 Migration of refugees from Mozambique to Tanzania to avoid civil war.
3 Migration in Peru from the Andes to Lima to escape poverty in the countryside.

Example	Distance:	Duration:	Decision:
	Internal or international?	Temporary or Permanent?	Voluntary or forced?
1	International		Voluntary
2	International	Temporary	
3		Permanent	Voluntary

1. Permanent. 2. Forced. 3. Internal.

6.6 International migration

International migration happens all over the world. The United Nations estimates that 100 million people are living in a different country from the one they were born in.

Key Point

Most international migrants move in search of a better life. Some move to be with family and friends, others move because they have no choice.

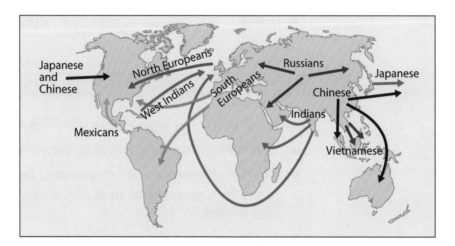

Fig. 6.6 International migration.

The most important international migrations in the 20th century included:
- Northern and Southern Europeans, Mexicans, Japanese and Chinese to the USA.
- West Indians and Indians to the UK.
- Russians and Indians to Africa.

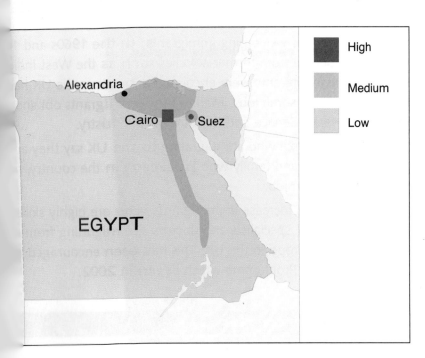

he map shows the population distribution in Egypt.

Describe the distribution of Egypt's population. (3)

Give two reasons for the location of the most dense area of population. (2)

gypt's population is 69.1 million, it is expected to reach 100 million by 2025.

Describe two problems that a rapidly growing population causes. (2)

Suggest methods that the Egyptian government could use to control
population growth. (3)

Immigration into the UK

About 300 000 migrants arrive in the UK each year, some with temporary or permanent visas, some as asylum seekers.

The population of the UK has been predicted to peak
Two-thirds of the increase is expected to come from

The UK has a history of welcoming immigrants. In th
the UK received people from former colonies such a
and Pakistan. The immigrants were encouraged bec
shortage of people for some jobs. Many of the imm
in the National Health Service and the transport ind

Now, many of the people who are migrating to the
moving to join friends and family who are already
than to find a particular job.

Some people argue that international migration causes problems, while others say that it is beneficial for everyone involved.

There has also been an increase in immigrants who
Scientists, engineers, IT specialists and doctors are
Central and Eastern Europe to the UK. This has be
Highly Skilled Migrant Programme which began in

Arguments for migration to the UK

- Immigrants provide cheap labour for employe
- Skilled workers are found for jobs that are sh
- Immigrants send money to relatives, improvii
- If migrants return they take skills and experie country of origin.
- The UK's culture is enriched with diverse foo
- In the UK the foreign-born population pays into government revenue than it takes out.

1

2

Arguments against migration to the U

- Immigration leads to more racial prejudice over 100 000 racial incidents such as attack each year.
- Immigrants tend to have a lower status in and less skilled.
- Some immigrants find it hard to get acces
- Unemployment levels for some ethnic grou
- Skilled immigrants take their skills away fr

The process of educated migrants leaving their country of origin is known as 'brain drain'.

Progress Check

1 Why were people encouraged to migrate to the U
2 What is the Highly Skilled Migrant Programme?
3 How many migrants arrive in the UK every year?

le to do certain jobs. 2. It is a programme to encourage skilled

7 Settlement

The topics covered in this chapter are:

- Settlement site and situation
- Settlement patterns and functions
- Changing cities and urban challenges
- Urban land use models
- Settlement hierarchies
- House building

After studying this topic you should be able to:

- describe the location of a settlement and give reasons why it is there
- identify and explain the shape that a settlement makes on the ground
- understand settlement building and usage
- account for the changes that are happening in cities
- name urban land use models and understand how they are put together
- understand settlement hierarchies
- appreciate the problems involved in housing growing populations.

7.1 Settlement site and situation

The **site** of a settlement is its exact location.

The **situation** of a settlement is its location in relation to surrounding physical and human features.

Key Point
Site factors are the reasons why the original population of a settlement chose to locate their settlement there.

The factors can be divided into the following areas:

Water supply	Clean water is needed for drinking, cooking and cleaning.
Relief	Flat land is easier to build on than steep or hilly land.
Fuel	Wood or coal is needed to burn for cooking and heat.

Soil	Deep and fertile soil is needed for farming.
Defence	A hill top or a bend in a river provides a safe site against attackers.
Transport	A site on a crossroads, river or coast makes it easier to access other settlements.
Building materials	A good supply of wood or stone is needed for buildings.
Dry land	Land that doesn't flood.
Crossing point	Where it is easy to cross a river using a bridge or a ford makes a good site.

You can analyse the site factors for any settlement. A close look at an Ordnance Survey map should provide you with a number of clues as to why a settlement is sited there.

Progress Check

Complete these sentences using the words below.

1 The exact location of a settlement is its _____.

2 The location of a settlement in relation to other settlements is known as its _____.

3 The shape of land is called _____.

situation   relief   site

1. Site. 2. Situation. 3. Relief.

7.2 Settlement patterns and functions

Settlement patterns

Key Point   The pattern of a settlement is the shape of the settlement.

Nucleated settlements have buildings that are grouped together. This might be for defensive reasons, social reasons or because of site factors such as a crossroads or being on a piece of high land away from floods.

Fig. 7.1 Settlement patterns.

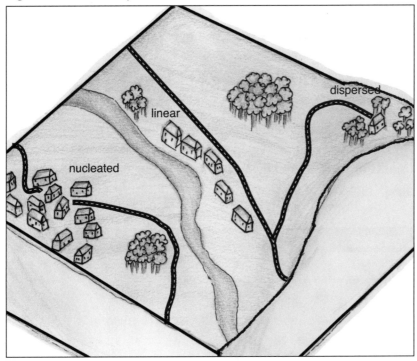

Linear settlements have buildings that are in a line. Linear settlements often follow the shape of the land, along a valley floor or a coastline. Transport routes such as roads, rivers, canals and railway lines have linear settlements built along them.

Dispersed settlements have buildings that are spread out over a wide area. A farmhouse in the middle of fields is a dispersed settlement. Another reason for dispersed settlements might be a harsh environment where it is difficult to live, for example in a mountainous region.

Settlement functions

The function of a settlement is the reason why it was built in the first place and the uses that people have for it today.

Settlements have more than one function and the functions of settlements are constantly changing. Many settlements in the UK are changing from having an industrial function to a service function, which might be tourism or shopping.

Residential	Settlements provide a place for people to live.
Administrative	Settlements have authorities who run local and national services.
Industrial	Many settlements have factories that produce manufactured goods.
Commercial	Most settlements have shops where people buy and sell goods.
Services	Settlements have services that people need, such as schools and hospitals.
Tourism	Some settlements are used by people for leisure and recreation.

Progress Check

True or false?

1 Nucleated settlements are grouped closely together.
2 Linear settlements often follow a road or a river.
3 The function of a settlement is the shape that it makes on the ground.

1. True. 2. True. 3. False.

7.3 Changing cities and urban challenges

Changes are often made to solve a problem. For each solution there will be people who like the changes and others who don't.

Cities in MEDCs and LEDCs are dynamic places – they are constantly changing. In MEDC cities new developments can be seen in the CBD (central business district), inner city and at the edge of the built-up area.

The London Docklands

Fig. 7.2 London Docklands.

The **London Docklands** used to be the busiest docks in the world. By 1981 ships had become too large to reach the docks and a new container dock had been opened further downstream at Tilbury. The docks were forced to close, leading to serious problems for this inner city area. Some 13 000 people lost their jobs. Most people lived in 19th century terraced houses which were small and in need of repair. Roads were narrow and there was a lack of public transport. The closure of the docks had created large areas of derelict land.

To solve the problems the government created the **London Docklands Development Corporation** (LDDC). The LDDC was given money to make improvements in the London Docklands area and to attract companies who would build new houses and create new jobs.

Key Point

The LDDC operated between 1981 and 1998. In this time the London Docklands was transformed.

The LDDC's successes

Canary Wharf tower on the Isle of Dogs, in the centre of the London Docklands, is Europe's largest office development and Britain's tallest building at 245 metres. It cost £4.4 billion to build, covers 30 hectares and 13 500 people work there.

- £10 billion has been spent on the London Docklands.
- 600 hectares of derelict land have been improved.
- 90 km of new roads have been built.
- 80 000 new jobs have been created.
- 24 000 new homes have been built.
- 100 000 trees have been planted.
- 130 hectares of parks have been created.
- Cultural venues such as the Docklands Arena have been opened.
- London Docklands is used for sporting events including rowing regattas and power boat racing.

Problems with the LDDC

- Many local people had to leave the area when old housing was demolished.
- The traditional 'East Ender' community spirit has been lost as people no longer know each other.
- Most of the new homes are too expensive for the local people to buy.
- Most of the jobs that have been created are high-tech, media or business jobs. Local people do not have the skills to work in this type of employment.
- There is a lack of some services such as hospitals and care for the elderly.

Progress Check

1 Why did the docks in the London Docklands close down?
2 What type of jobs did the LDDC create?
3 Why might ex-dock workers be unhappy with the new jobs?

1. The ships became too big and a new dock was opened at Tilbury. 2. Jobs in business, finance and the media. 3. Ex-dock workers are unlikely to have the skills to work in these types of jobs.

7.4 Urban land use models

Key Point
An urban land use model is a way of showing how land is used in a city. Models are designed to simplify a real situation in order to make it easier to understand.

Burgess was a geographer who created a land use model for Chicago in 1924. His ideas were so good that his model has become the standard used to explain the land use of cities in MEDCs.

Shops and offices are prepared to pay more money than anyone else to locate in the CBD. This is where they will make the most profit because this is where most people come to shop.

At the centre of the model is the **Central Business District** (CBD). This is where most of the shops and offices are found.

Surrounding the CBD is the **inner city**. This is a mixture of low quality housing and industry. In the UK most inner cities were built in the 19th century. The housing was built close to the factories because transport was expensive and few people had access to it.

Surrounding the inner city are the **suburbs**. These are the zones of medium quality and high quality housing which were built from the early 20th century up to the present day.

The zone in transition and the zone of low quality housing make up the inner city on Burgess's model.

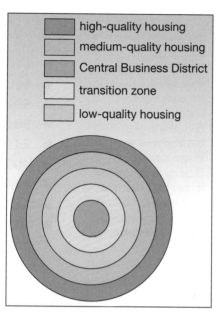

high-quality housing
medium-quality housing
Central Business District
transition zone
low-quality housing

Fig. 7.3 Burgess's urban land use model.

The suburbs grew because people moved out of the inner city looking for a better quality of life on the outskirts of the city. With improvements in transport in the 20th century people no longer had to live close to where they worked. Here land was cheaper, there was more space, less traffic, cleaner air and more modern housing.

A shanty town is an area of housing in an LEDC city which has been built by the people who live there on land they do not own. Most of the houses are made from waste materials. Shanty towns are unplanned and have no running water, electricity or sewage system when they are first built.

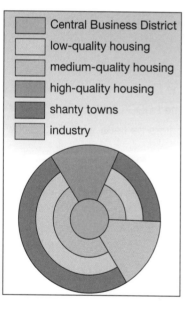

Central Business District
low-quality housing
medium-quality housing
high-quality housing
shanty towns
industry

Fig. 7.4 An urban land use model for an LEDC city.

Land use in LEDC cities is different from MEDC cities. The most obvious difference is that the quality of housing improves as you get closer to the CBD. At the edge of most LEDC cities you find shanty towns.

The most highly paid jobs in LEDC cities tend to be found in the CBD. This is where the offices of many multinational companies are located. The centre is also where you would find the best shops and entertainment. As transport is often expensive and unreliable in LEDC cities, higher income groups prefer to live nearer the CBD than at the edge.

Progress Check

1 Where are shops and offices found in Burgess's model?
2 Which model has low quality housing at the edge of the urban area?
3 Why do geographers use urban land use models?

1. In the CBD. 2. The LEDC urban model. 3. To make urban areas easier to understand.

7.5 Settlement hierarchies

Settlements can be put into an order of importance using a range of criteria including their size, population, proximity to other settlements, number of services and sphere of influence.

Services are facilities that help people, such as shops, schools, hospitals and libraries. A settlement at the bottom of a hierarchy has few services, whereas a settlement at the top of the hierarchy has a lot. This is because there are not enough people to use many services in a small settlement.

> Hierarchies are drawn as pyramids because the higher a settlement is in a hierarchy the fewer there will be of that type of settlement.

> The distance people are prepared to travel to a service is known as the range.

> The number of people required to keep a service running is known as the threshold. For example, a village shop has a threshold of 300 people and a large supermarket has a threshold of 50 000 people.

Fig. 7.5 A settlement hierarchy.

importance ↗ — *number ↘*

- Mega-city or Capital
- City
- Town
- Village
- Hamlet

Not only does the resident population of a settlement use the services, but as a settlement becomes more important a greater number of people are prepared to travel to that settlement, increasing the services that are found there.

The **sphere of influence** of a settlement is the area affected by it. The higher up the settlement hierarchy a settlement is, the larger its sphere of influence will be because people will come from further afield to use the services that are available.

Places where people shop can also be put into a hierarchy. The criteria for the hierarchy include the size of the shop, how many people shop there, how often they shop there, how far people are prepared to travel to shop there, the sort of goods that are sold there, and the value of the goods that are sold there.

The places in which people shop that are at the top of the shopping hierarchy are known as **high order centres**; those at the bottom are known as **low order centres**.

High order centres contain high order shops which sell high order goods, including clothing, jewellery, furniture and electrical items. High order centres sell goods that are expensive, that people don't buy very often, and that people are prepared to travel quite far to buy.

- CBD of a large urban area or A regional shopping centre
- Retail park with warehouse stores
- High streets
- Supermarkets and superstores
- Newsagents, corner shops and petrol-station shops

> A department store is an example of a high order shop.

Fig. 7.6 A shopping hierarchy.

Low order centres contain low order shops that sell low order goods, including bread, milk and newspapers. Low order centres sell goods that are cheap, that people buy every day, and that people are prepared to travel only a short distance for.

Progress Check

1 Put these settlements, shops and services into the right places in the table below.

city   village   newsagent   shoe shop   university   primary school

	Settlement	Shop	Service
High order			
Low order			

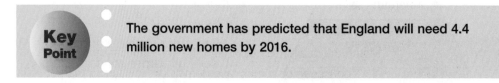

	Settlement	Shop	Service
High order	city	shoe shop	university
Low order	village	newsagent	primary school

7.6   House building

The demand for new housing is growing, and the problem is finding enough space. There is often a conflict between the people who want to build new housing and the people who want to protect the land from being built on.

Key Point

The government has predicted that England will need 4.4 million new homes by 2016.

Why new homes are needed:
- People are leaving home at a younger age.
- People are waiting longer before they get married.
- There are more single people, either as a result of divorce or because they prefer to live alone.
- People are living longer.

The south-east of England has the greatest need for new housing. This is because people are migrating from the north of the UK to the south-east of England in search of jobs and a better quality of life.

The government has highlighted four areas in the south-east where they plan to build over 200 000 homes.

Fig. 7.7 Four areas for new housing in the South East.

Arguments for new housing

Brownfield sites are areas of land that have previously been developed and are now derelict or unused.

- The demand for housing in the south-east makes house prices there the highest in the UK.
- There is a shortage of affordable housing in the south-east. If the new housing isn't built, key workers like nurses, teachers and fire-fighters will not be able to buy homes in the region.
- The government will make sure that as much new housing as possible is built on brownfield sites.

Arguments against new housing

Greenbelt land is land that surrounds a settlement, that has been protected from development.

- There are fears that services such as schools and hospitals will not be able to keep up with the increase in the number of people when new houses are built.
- Thousands of hectares of greenbelt land could be lost.
- The Council for the Protection of Rural England has said that the environment simply cannot take the scale of growth proposed.
- People should be encouraged to live elsewhere in the country.
- There are inner city areas and regions in the North of England where housing is standing empty.

Progress Check

Match the headlines below with the correct location.
1 Thousands of homes face demolition as housing market collapses.
2 Schools suffer recruitment crisis as teachers struggle to buy homes.
3 Is this the end of our 'green and pleasant land'?

south-east   north   the UK

1. North. 2. South-east. 3. The UK

Practice questions

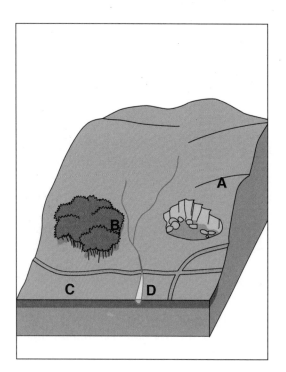

1 What is the site of a settlement? **(1)**

2 Describe sites A, B, C and D in the diagram. **(4)**

3 Why is C the best site? **(4)**

4 Why do shanty towns in LEDC cities tend to be found at sites like A and D? **(4)**

8 Economic activities

The topics covered in this chapter are:

- **Economic activities**
- **Farming**
- **Farming in the UK**
- **Farming and the environment**
- **Traditional and modern industry**
- **Industry and the environment**
- **Tourist industry and impacts of tourism**

After studying this topic you should be able to

- identify primary, secondary, tertiary and quaternary activities
- describe and explain the human and physical influences on farming
- account for the changes in UK farming
- understand the effect that farming has on the environment
- describe and explain the rise and fall of heavy manufacturing industry in MEDCs
- give reasons for the location of modern manufacturing industry
- evaluate the impacts of industry on the environment
- describe and explain how shopping is changing
- identify the characteristics of the tourist industry
- understand the positive and negative effects of tourism.

8.1 Economic activities

> **Key Point**
>
> Economic activities are ways that people make their living. They can be divided into four types.

Raw materials are natural resources that industry uses to turn into finished products through the manufacturing process.

Services are facilities that help people.

- **Primary activity** – the extraction of raw materials from the ground or sea. This includes mining, quarrying, fishing, farming and forestry.
- **Secondary activity** – making things from raw materials. This includes processing, manufacturing, assembly and construction.
- **Tertiary activity** – providing people with services. This includes shops, offices, schools, hospitals, transport, leisure and tourism.
- **Quaternary activity** – research and development. This includes information technology, biotechnology and communications.

8.2 Farming

Key Point

Farming is the growing of crops and the rearing of animals.

There are three main types of farming:

- **Arable** – growing crops, e.g. wheat, barley, fruit, vegetables, oil seed rape.
- **Pastoral** – raising animals, e.g. cows, sheep, pigs, goats, chickens.
- **Mixed farming** – a combination of arable and pastoral farming.

You will also come across the following terms:

Intensive farming is producing a high output from a small area of land.
Extensive farming is producing a low output from a large area of land.

Commercial farming is farming to make profit from sales of produce.
Subsistence farming is farming to feed yourself and your family with your produce.

Nomadic farming is moving from place to place.
Sedentary farming is staying in a fixed location.

Farming is influenced by **human** and **physical factors** – these affect both the **type of farming** that happens in a particular location and the **success of a farm** from year to year.

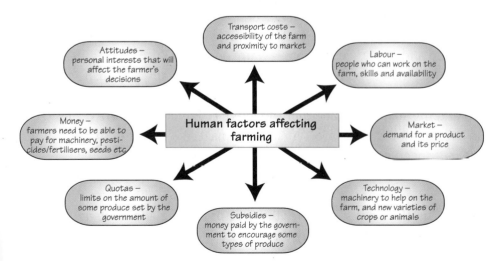

Human factors affecting farming:

- Transport costs – accessibility of the farm and proximity to market
- Attitudes – personal interests that will affect the farmer's decisions
- Labour – people who can work on the farm, skills and availability
- Money – farmers need to be able to pay for machinery, pesticides/fertilisers, seeds etc.
- Market – demand for a product and its price
- Quotas – limits on the amount of some produce set by the government
- Subsidies – money paid by the government to encourage some types of produce
- Technology – machinery to help on the farm, and new varieties of crops or animals

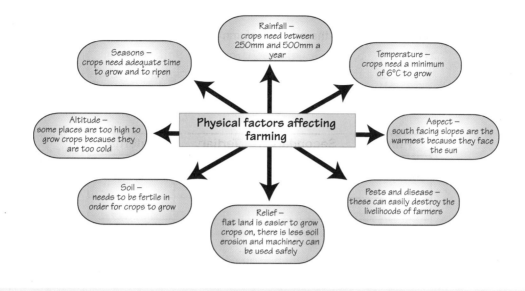

Progress Check

1 What is farming with animals known as?
2 What is the lowest temperature at which crops can survive?
3 Why do crops grow better on south-facing slopes?

1. Pastoral. 2. 6°C. 3. Because south-facing slopes get more sun, which helps the crops to grow and ripen.

8.3 Farming in the UK

Key Point

The location and success of farming in the UK is determined by a combination of human and physical factors.

The distribution of farming in the UK

- **Dairy farming** is found in the west of the UK. Here the land is flat, the soil is fertile and there is plenty of rain to guarantee a good amount of grass all year round.
- **Arable farming** is found in the east of the UK. The land is flat and the soil is deep and fertile. The climate is warm and fairly dry, which is ideal for crops like wheat and barley, which need sunny weather to ripen.
- **Sheep and beef cattle** are found in upland areas, where the land is steep and the soil tends to be thin and infertile. Temperatures are cooler than average and there is a lot of rain. This makes it difficult to grow crops, but sheep and some cattle thrive in this environment.
- **Market gardening** is the growing of crops such as fruit and vegetables. Most market gardening is found in greenhouses in the south-east of England. The climate is suitable for this type of farming and there are plenty of towns and cities to buy the produce.

How is farming changing in the UK?

More than 3 million people work in agriculture in the UK. The **UK is 80 per cent self-sufficient in food** – this means that we are able to grow nearly all the food that we need.

However, farming is in crisis. Farm incomes dropped by 72 per cent between 1995 and 2000. The number of farmers losing their jobs has been steadily increasing – 23 800 farmers lost their jobs in the year 2000.

Why is farming changing?

- Consumers want higher quality food, more choice of types of food and lower prices.
- There are increasing environmental and animal welfare regulations.
- Farming has been hit by diseases such as foot and mouth and BSE.
- The amount of support that farmers get from the European Union (EU) and the government has fallen.

The Common Agricultural Policy (CAP)

In the 1960s the EU was known as the European Economic Community (EEC).

In the 1960s the EU created the **CAP**. The aim of the CAP was to increase the amount farms produced and to improve the quality of life for farmers. A single market for agricultural produce throughout Europe was created. Prices were guaranteed and the EU promised to buy everything that the farmers could produce.

The CAP worked – farmers increased their production and their quality of life improved. However, the scheme became too successful. European farmers produced more food than Europe needed, so large mountains and lakes of produce built up, which were expensive to store and had to be sold off cheaply to the rest of the world.

The EU had to introduce a system of **quotas**, which were a maximum amount that they were prepared to buy from each farmer. The EU also began to pay farmers not to farm parts of their land – this was known as '**set aside**'. After 1992 the EU also cut the prices that it was paying for some produce.

With less support from the CAP, many farmers chose to change the way they used their land to make money. This is known as **diversification**.

Examples of diversification:
- campsites
- organic farms
- bed and breakfast
- paint ball games
- educational farms
- garden centres
- pick your own.

Other farmers are seeking alternative sources of income from their farms, such as setting up farmers' markets in local towns, or by receiving a government grant for protecting environmentally sensitive areas on their farms.

Progress Check

1 Where is sheep farming found in the UK?
2 What were the aims of the CAP?
3 Why did the EU introduce set aside?
4 How has diversification helped farmers in the UK?

1. In upland areas. 2. To increase produce and improve the quality of life for farmers. 3. Because farmers were producing more than the EU needed. 4. They make money from their land in other ways.

8.4 Farming and the environment

> **Key Point**
>
> Farming can have positive and negative effects on the environment.

Pesticides and fertilisers

The chemicals and techniques some farmers use cause pollution and affect wildlife. However, farming can also protect the countryside and actively conserve species and landscapes.

Pesticides are dangerous to people and wildlife. Conservationists say that pesticides reduce the number of insects in the countryside, this decreases the amount of food available to wild birds and other predators.

Fertilisers cause a type of pollution known as eutrophication. Nitrates are washed from fields into streams and rivers; these cause weeds and algae to grow so that they cover the surface of the water. This blocks out sunlight and uses up the oxygen so all the water life dies.

The United Nations has calculated that in LEDCs 25 million people a year are poisoned by pesticides.

Disappearing hedgerows

Farming has also changed the landscape. The most obvious change in the UK has been the loss of hedgerows as farmers merged several small fields into one large field. Between 1949 and 1990 over 330 000 km of hedgerow was lost. This produces monotonous views and leads to the disappearance of valuable wildlife habitats.

Irrigation

Irrigation is any method of providing water to crops. Traditional methods could be a bucket on a pole, known as a *shaduf* in Egypt; high-tech methods include boom irrigation, where crops are given a constant supply of water pumped out of a rotating arm.

Irrigation schemes in LEDCs help to keep crops watered and maintain high yields. However, as the water evaporates from the fields, salts and minerals are left. The build-up of deposits can be so great that the land is poisoned and it becomes impossible to grow crops there.

Improving the environment

Government schemes to protect the environment include the Environmentally Sensitive Areas (ESAs) Scheme, the Woodland Management Scheme and the Countryside Stewardship Scheme.

Farming can help the environment. In the UK farmers are paid by the government to protect the environment. Over 10 000 farmers are involved in the Environmentally Sensitive Areas Scheme, and 7000 in the Countryside Stewardship Scheme. For example, farmers are paid 50 per cent of the cost of replanting hedgerows.

In 2000 the total length of hedgerows in the UK was 450 000 km. Conservationists now think it will not be long before the total amount of hedgerows in the UK begins to increase.

Progress Check

True or false?

1 Hedgerows create a monotonous landscape.
2 Irrigation can leave salt and minerals on the ground surface, making it impossible to grow crops.
3 The UK government is paying farmers to protect the environment.

1. False. 2. True. 3. True.

8.5 Traditional industry

Key Point

Industry means making things from natural resources – this is also known as manufacturing.

The Industrial Revolution

Industry can also refer to any commercial activity, e.g. the hotel industry.

The **Industrial Revolution** happened during the second half of the 18th century in the UK. During the Industrial Revolution a series of inventions led to the development of large-scale manufacturing involving many people working in factories.

The first factories made **iron, steel** and **textiles**. During the early 19th century, ship building and manufacturing related to the railways became increasingly important. Iron, steel, textiles, railway and shipbuilding industries are known as **traditional manufacturing** or **heavy industry**.

Before the Industrial Revolution manufacturing was done by individuals in their own homes – this is known as cottage industry.

Factories at this time used steam power. Coal was important as it provided the fuel for the steam engines. Most factories were built close to the sources of coal, which was heavy and expensive to transport.

The other important raw materials were limestone and iron ore because they were used in the steel-making process along with coal.

Core regions/countries for traditional manufacturing:

- UK regions were on the coalfields of south Wales, the Midlands, north-east England and central Scotland. There were also wool mills in Yorkshire and cotton mills in Lancashire.
- The main industrial regions in Europe were the Rhine/Ruhr region in Germany, including the urban areas of Cologne, Dusseldorf and Dortmund; and northern France, particularly the city of Lille.
- In the USA, industry developed in the north-east, New England and a belt running from the Great Lakes to the Atlantic coast, taking in the cities of Chicago, Detroit, Pittsburgh, Cleveland and Buffalo.

Deindustrialisation

Towards the second half of the 20th century the traditional manufacturing regions suffered from a process called **deindustrialisation**. This is a combination of a decline in the output of manufactured products and a decrease in the number of people employed. Sales fell, costs increased and factories were forced to close.

There are a number of reasons for deindustrialisation:

- Raw materials were beginning to run out or were becoming increasingly expensive to extract.
- Companies closed old-fashioned factories which were expensive to run.
- More efficient manufacturing techniques using computers and robots were developed, which required fewer people.
- Competition increased from other countries that were able to manufacture products more cheaply than the traditional manufacturing countries.
- Globalisation led to companies closing factories in MEDCs where production costs such as wages were high, and opening new factories in LEDCs where costs were much lower.

Globalisation is the spread of economic activity worldwide.

Progress Check

Study the map and then answer these questions.

1 Why did the iron and steel industry develop in south Wales?

2 What happened to most of the steel once it had been made?

3 Why do you think Abergavenny didn't grow as much as Cardiff or Swansea?

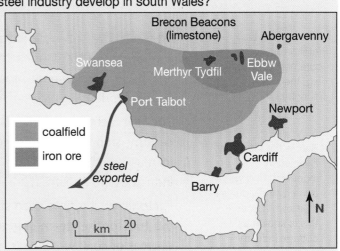

1. South Wales has supplies of coal, iron ore and limestone, the raw materials for steel.
2. It was exported. 3. It was not on a coal or iron ore field and it was not on the coast.

8.6 Modern industry

Modern industry includes traditional heavy industry. It also involves light manufacturing and high-tech industry.

Light manufacturing produces electrical goods, parts for vehicles, food, clothing and footwear.

High-tech industry is electronics, information technology and biotechnology.

> **Key Point**
>
> Modern industry is 'footloose', which means that it is not tied to one particular location.

> Industrial estates attract more light industry; business parks include offices as well as manufacturing; science parks contain more high-tech industries and are usually owned or supported by a local university.

> Greenfield sites have not been built on before; and are usually on the edge of towns and cities.

Modern industry tends to locate in industrial estates, business parks or science parks. These are areas where a number of companies are located.

Modern industry looks for certain characteristics when choosing a location:

- An educated and skilled workforce.
- People looking for part-time employment.
- Good transport links, particularly motorways and airports.
- Proximity to universities and research establishments.
- Government incentives, such as those found in areas where industry previously has been declining.
- A greenfield site.
- A pleasant environment with attractions nearby.
- A good quality of life to attract the best possible employees to the area.
- Many people in the area to buy the goods.

> **Progress Check**
>
> 1 What is the difference between a business park and a science park?
> 2 What does 'footloose' mean?
> 3 Why does high-tech industry locate on greenfield sites?
>
> 1. A business park has light manufacturing and offices, a science park has connections to a local university. 2. Not tied to a particular location. 3. Because they are a pleasant place to work and the best employees will be attracted to work there. Also it is easier to build the correct type of building and is close to transport links.

8.7 Industry and the environment

> **Key Point**
>
> Industry causes air, water and land pollution. The effects of the pollution caused by industry can be local, national or global.

Pollution is anything that is introduced to the environment that causes damage.

Air pollution

Burning fossil fuels (coal, oil and gas) releases carbon dioxide, sulphur and nitrogen oxides.

Carbon dioxide is a **greenhouse gas**, which means that it contributes to **global warming**. Global warming could lead to climate change and sea level rises around the world.

Sulphur and nitrogen oxides are transformed in the atmosphere into sulphuric and nitric acid, which falls as **acid rain**. Acid rain harms water life in rivers and lakes; it has been blamed for causing trees to die, particularly in Scandinavia, and it increases the chemical weathering of some buildings.

Other examples of air pollution include **chlorofluorocarbons** (CFCs) and **photochemical smog**. CFCs used to be in aerosols and fridges. These gases destroy the ozone layer, allowing more ultraviolet radiation from the sun to reach the Earth, leading to a greater risk of skin cancer for people.

Photochemical smog is created by a chemical reaction between sunlight and gases from industry and vehicles. It causes breathing difficulties, eye irritation and can kill.

Water pollution

Water containing chemicals released by industry is known as effluent.

Toxic chemicals have been released into rivers, streams, lakes and seas, damaging water life. One of the biggest causes of water pollution in the sea is spills from oil tankers.

Dzerzhinsk in Russia, the home of Russia's chemical industry, is one of the most polluted places on Earth. Some 1150 sources of pollution have been identified there. A lake on the outskirts of the town has been found to contain cancer-causing chemicals and other toxic chemicals at a level 17 million times greater than safety limits allow.

Land pollution

Land can become contaminated by industry. When industry closes down, land can be left derelict, which is an eyesore and dangerous to people and wildlife. Industry sometimes creates spoil heaps, piles of waste materials.

In 1966 in the Welsh mining village of Aberfan, a spoil tip collapsed and slid downhill, killing 144 people.

Solutions

Steps have been taken internationally and nationally to reduce the effects that industry has on the environment.

In 1992 the first United Nations Earth Summit was held in Rio de Janeiro, Brazil. Treaties were created to prevent global warming and protect biodiversity. In 1997 a Climate Conference was held in Kyoto, Japan. Countries were encouraged to sign an agreement to reduce their carbon dioxide emissions.

In the UK laws have been passed to prevent industry polluting the environment. The UK government follows the principle of 'the polluter pays'. This means that the people responsible for making a mess are required by law to pay for it to be cleaned up.

> Biodiversity is the variety of plant and animal species.

Progress Check

1 Name three gases that pollute the atmosphere.
2 Where is the most polluted place in the world?
3 What can be done to reduce pollution?

1. Sulphur dioxide, nitrogen dioxide, CFCs. 2. Dzerzhinsk in Russia. 3. Countries can sign global treaties and national governments can pass laws to prevent people from polluting.

8.8 Tourist industry

> The global expansion in tourism has been made possible by cheaper air travel, rising personal incomes and more leisure time.

Tourism is a tertiary activity because the service provided is helping people to go on holiday.

In 2000 there were 697 million tourists worldwide. This is expected to grow to over 1 billion by 2010. Tourism accounts for 8 per cent of world trade, and this, too, is expected to increase.

Tourist destinations

Tourists choose destinations for a number of reasons:
- **Coasts** – usually cooler in summer than inland locations, people enjoy water sports in the sea or relaxing on a beach.
- **Climate** – people choose holiday destinations with warm, sunny weather, particularly to escape a cold winter at home.
- **Scenery** – locations with breath-taking views or stunning scenery are always popular.
- **Culture** – discerning tourists like to visit places of historical interest or destinations with a culture that is different from their own.
- **Entertainment and activities** – most tourists like things to do and attractions to visit.

Tourism in the UK

Tourism started in the UK in the Victorian era. People visited spa towns like Buxton or Bath, where they would drink the water and have a healthy break. With the development of the railways, people took holidays on the coast at places like Blackpool and Brighton. People also travelled abroad on cultural holidays in Europe.

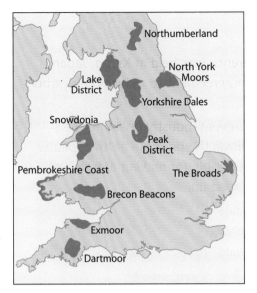

Fig. 8.1 National Parks in the UK.

In 1949 the Countryside Act created Britain's first National Parks. Initially there were 10 of these, including the Lake District, Snowdonia, Dartmoor, the Yorkshire Dales and the Peak District. They were created to preserve and enhance areas of outstanding natural beauty and to promote people's enjoyment of the countryside.

Today the most popular holiday destinations in the UK are still coastal resorts. National Parks are extremely popular, as are city breaks to places like York. Most tourists who come to the UK from overseas spend the majority of their time in cultural locations such as London, Oxford, Bath and Stratford upon Avon. They also go to the National Parks as well as visiting Wales, Scotland and Northern Ireland.

International tourism

With the development of affordable air travel, international tourism took off in the 1970s. People began to go on package holidays. The Mediterranean became a popular package holiday destination and countries such as Spain and Greece experienced a rapid growth in their tourism industry.

> Package holidays are trips where everything is arranged for you by a tour company.

Package holidays have become less fashionable recently. People are prepared to travel to more distant locations such as the USA, Mexico, Thailand and Kenya. These are known as long haul destinations because of the time it takes to get there from the UK. The tourists travel to experience the different culture, landscapes and wildlife of these countries.

Progress Check

True or false?

1 Globally, tourism is declining.
2 Most tourists to the UK go to the coast, national parks and places of cultural interest.
3 A long haul destination is a holiday where everything is arranged for you.

1. False. 2. True. 3. False.

8.9 Impacts of tourism

Key Point

Tourism can have positive and negative effects. It needs to be carefully managed so that the features that originally attracted tourists are not destroyed by the scale of tourism that develops.

Positive effects of tourism

- Jobs are created for local people.
- Local people make money from making or selling souvenirs.
- Local people benefit from the facilities that are provided for the tourists.
- Infrastructure that is built for tourists benefits local people.
- Money generated by tourism can be used to pay for the conservation of the environment or heritage sites.
- Culture and traditions are preserved and valued.

Negative effects of tourism

- Jobs are seasonal, so people are out of work for some of the year.
- Local people are excluded from tourist developments.
- Money that is made from tourism goes to multinational companies such as tour operators, hotel chains and airlines, not local people.
- Tourist developments can damage fragile ecosystems, large numbers of tourists can disturb the environment and wildlife.
- Local culture and traditions are changed as people are exposed to new ideas and ways of life brought by tourists.

Managing tourism in Kenya

> Some 150 000 British tourists visit Kenya each year.

Kenya receives approximately 1 million visitors a year.

Tourism is vital for Kenya's economy. It is Kenya's largest source of money from other countries.

Tourists are attracted to Kenya by its culture, beautiful scenery, Indian Ocean coastline and wildlife. A trip to Kenya would not be complete without a safari in one of Kenya's 50 national parks and game reserves.

Fig. 8.2 Kenya's tourist attractions.

The benefits of tourism to Kenya

- Jobs are provided by the tourist industry, from being a tour guide to a gardener in a hotel.
- Income that is made from tourists visiting the national parks and game reserves is used to protect the wildlife.
- Profits from tourism can be used to help Kenya develop by investing in services and industry.

The problems caused by tourism in Kenya

- Large hotels have been built on the south-east coast near Mombasa, natural vegetation has been cleared and wildlife has disappeared.
- Tourists kill coral by walking on it and churning up mud from the sea bed in motor boats.
- Sea turtle nesting sites on beaches are being disturbed.
- Tourist buses in the national parks disturb wildlife by creating dust and noise. This causes the animals to leave the parks and destroy local crops.
- Local people such as the Masai have lost traditional land where they used to graze their cattle.
- Some Masai have become dependent on selling souvenirs and entertaining tourists for their income.

Solutions to the problems

Kenya is developing **ecotourist** holidays.

Key Point

Ecotourism is tourism that protects and conserves the environment.

Ecotourism also ensures that local people are not disadvantaged by tourism and that they are fairly paid for any contribution that they make.

An example of ecotourism in Kenya is the Turtle Bay Beach Club. This is an ecotourist hotel near Mombasa. Tourists are encouraged to travel around the area on bicycles. The beach is shared with the sea turtles. Safaris are done on foot and the tourists stay in solar-powered tents. A percentage of the income from tourism is donated to a local orphanage, which the tourists are encouraged to visit.

Progress Check

1 Name three Kenyan national parks on the border with Tanzania.
2 Why are animals leaving some national parks?
3 How can an ecotourist holiday help to keep the animals in the national parks?

1. Masai Mara National Reserve, Amboseli National Park, Tsavo National Park. 2. They are driven away by the noise and dust from tourist buses. 3. Ecotourism protects wildlife, as people are encouraged to do safaris on foot so that they do not disturb the wildlife.

Practice questions

1 Match the labels with the farm pictures. **(10)**

Pastoral   Arable
Rich soil   Sheep
Too much rain   Hilly
Cold winters   Flat
Plenty of sun   Wheat

The map shows the location of high-tech industry in the UK.

2 Describe the location of high-tech industry in the UK. **(4)**

3 Give three reasons why most high-tech industry is found along the M4 motorway. **(3)**

9 Development

The topics covered in this chapter are:

- **What is development?**
- **Measuring development and obstacles to development**
- **International trade and transnational corporations**
- **Aid and debt**
- **Appropriate development**

After studying this topic you should be able to:

- identify MEDCs and LEDCs
- recognise the methods used to measure development
- understand why some countries are more developed than others
- understand that development can have a bad side as well as a good side
- know how trade affects development
- identify transnational corporations and evaluate their impact
- explain the rapid economic growth of newly industrialised countries
- recognise different types of aid and explain examples of appropriate aid
- understand the causes and consequences of international debt.

9.1 What is development?

The simplest definition of development is 'the process of countries becoming richer'.

However, development involves more than just the wealth of a country. A fuller definition would include descriptions of the population using concepts like standard of living and quality of life.

The term **'Standard of living'** is the material well-being of a person: the value of their possessions and savings, the type of home they live in and whether they own items such as a washing machine, television, car, telephone and computer.

'Quality of life' is the general well-being of a person. It includes standard of living, but is also affected by education, health care, services, utilities, environment, and social, political and religious freedom that a person experiences.

Key Point

Development is therefore the improvements in standard of living and quality of life that follow from a country becoming richer.

The countries of the world can be divided into three groups according to their levels of development. The names that we use for each type of country have changed, although most people use both the old and the new names.

> **Key Point**
>
> The new names recognise that every country is developing, but that some countries are more developed than others.

Most MEDCs are found towards the north of the world and most LEDCs are found towards the south. Japan, Australia and New Zealand are amongst countries that are an exception to this rule (they are MEDCs in the southern hemisphere). Sometimes MEDCs are described as belonging to the 'rich north' and LEDCs to the 'poor south'.

Remember that these definitions refer to the whole country. Within countries there are vast differences in standards of living and quality of life in the population.

Old names	World regions	New names
First World	Western Europe North America Australasia	More Economically Developed Countries (MEDCs)
Second World	Russia China Eastern Europe	Countries in transition
Third World	Africa Asia South America	Less Economically Developed Countries (LEDCs)

Fig. 9.1 World levels of economic development.

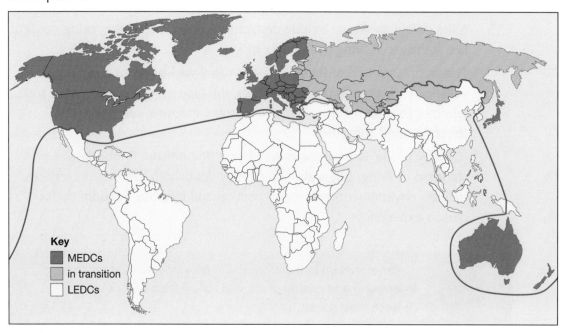

Key
- MEDCs
- in transition
- LEDCs

Facts about world development

- 1 in 5 of the world's population lives in the rich north, yet the rich north uses four-fifths of the world's resources.
- The richest three people in the world have more money and property than all the money and property owned by the poorest 600 million people.
- 100 million people in the world are homeless.
- 900 million people have no education.
- 880 million people do not have enough to eat.
- 30 per cent of the world's population can read.
- 1 per cent have been to university.
- 1 per cent own a computer.
- The cost of providing basic healthcare and food for everyone in the world would be less than is spent in Europe and the USA on pet food every year.

Progress Check

1 What is development?

2 Which countries in the south of the world are MEDCs?

3 Why is it misleading to think that everyone is well off if they live in an MEDC?

1. The improvements in quality of life and standard of living that follow as a country becomes richer. 2. Australia, Japan and New Zealand. 3. Wealth is not shared out evenly between everyone, so in a country there could be a few very rich people and many poor people.

9.2 Measuring development

 Key Point

There are many ways of measuring the development of a country. Each method is known as an 'indicator of development'.

Figures for GDP and income are given in US$ to make it easier to compare countries.

Gross Domestic Product (GDP) per capita

The total value of goods and services produced by a country, divided by its population. GDP is the most commonly used indicator of wealth, however it does hide differences in wealth within a country.

Gross National Product (GNP) per capita

GNP is the same as GDP, with the profits from international flows of money included.

Income

The average amount of money earned per person. This is only useful when you know how expensive things are to buy in the country.

Adult Literacy

This is the percentage of people in a country over the age of 18 who can read and write.

Imports & Exports

The goods that a country buys from other countries, and the goods that a

To be a good measure of development the data related to an indicator must be easy to find out. It must also be possible for it to be used to compare all countries.

country sells to other countries. LEDCs tend to sell cheap raw materials to MEDCs and buy expensive manufactured goods from MEDCs.

Employment structure

The percentage of people in a country who work in primary, secondary, tertiary and quaternary industry. LEDCs tend to have a greater percentage of people working in primary and secondary industry than MEDCs.

Poverty

The percentage of people in a country living on less than 60p a day.

Life Expectancy

The average number of years a person will live in a country. People tend to live longer in MEDCs than LEDCs.

Infant mortality

The number of babies that die before they are one year old per 1000 people.

People per doctor

The average number of people per doctor.

Calorific intake

The average amount of food each person eats expressed in calories. The World Health Organisation (WHO) recommends that a man should eat 2500 calories a day and a woman should eat 2000 calories a day.

Population indicators

Population indicators such as the population, population density, population growth, fertility rate, birth rate and death rate are also useful measures of development. These are explained in Chapter 6. Birth rates and death rates are particularly helpful in understanding the quality of healthcare in a country, as well as whether the conditions in a country lead to people having more or fewer children.

A large or a fast-growing population can be blamed for causing underdevelopment. Sometimes this is a mistake because there might be other reasons for underdevelopment. The large or growing population could be a symptom of the problems rather than the cause.

The Human Development Index (HDI)

The HDI was created by the United Nations Development Programme in 1990. Three indicators – income per person, adult literacy and life expectancy – are added together and worked out as a score between 0 and 1. The closer to 1, the higher the level of development.

Progress Check

1 Which indicators measure health?
2 What are the characteristics of a useful indicator?
3 Why is the HDI a better measure than GDP?

1. Life expectancy, infant mortality, people per doctor, calorific intake. 2. It must be easy to measure and easy to compare between countries. 3. The HDI tells you about wealth, health and education, GDP just tells you about wealth.

9.3 Obstacles to development

One of the most crucial questions facing us in the 21st century is why some countries are more developed than others.

Key Point — Knowing why some countries are more developed than others is one step closer to solving the problem of the huge inequalities between people on the planet.

Obstacles to development can be divided into human and physical factors.

Physical factors

- **Climate** – extremes of climate make development difficult. The polar regions and desert regions such as the Sahara or the interior of Australia are examples.
- **Relief** – a very mountainous landscape inhibits development. A well-known example would be the Himalayan region in Tibet, but the Andes in South America have the same effect.
- **Water supply** – arid areas or deserts restrict development, and countries that suffer frequent flooding such as Bangladesh, have development problems.
- **Ecosystems** – dense forests make development difficult – for example, the Amazon rainforest in Brazil.
- **Natural resources** – a country that has plenty of natural resources is at an economic advantage compared to a country that does not. Raw materials such as coal, oil, gas and iron ore can be extracted and used to increase the wealth of the country.

Human factors

- **Colonialism** – in the 15th and 16th centuries, European countries expanded their territories by taking control of countries in North and South America, Africa and Asia. The colonial powers used the countries they had taken over mainly for raw materials. They exported agricultural products, timber and ores, amongst other goods, from the colonies. These were used in manufacturing in the European country and often the manufactured goods were imported back to the colony.

  This system had two effects. The immediate effect was to strip wealth from the colony and increase the wealth of the country in control. The long-term effect was to create a system of employment and international trade which continues today and maintains some of the unequal flows of wealth around the world.

Some civil wars could be blamed on colonialism. European countries divided up land between them and created countries, with little thought to which groups owned particular areas of land originally.

Total world debt stands at about $354 billion. Africa spends four times more on paying back its debts than it does on healthcare.

- **Civil war** – a number of LEDCs have suffered from wars between opposing groups within the country. Money that could be spent on development is put into the war. In addition, the country cannot grow economically while fighting is going on.
- **Debt** – MEDCs have lent money to LEDCs to help them to develop. This was either done directly between two countries, or it has been done through international organisations such as the World Bank or the International Monetary Fund (IMF). LEDCs are therefore spending money on paying back the loans rather than on development.
- **Health and disease** – development in some countries has been held back by the prevalence of disease. Resources which could be spent on helping the country to develop are diverted to treat diseases.

Cholera, malaria and AIDS are three of the most serious diseases facing LEDCs today. Malaria, a tropical disease carried by mosquitoes, kills about two million people each year. Cholera is carried in dirty water – about 120000 people die each year from disease spread by unclean water. AIDS is out of control in some LEDCs. 1.4 million people are infected with the HIV virus in Africa every year.

Progress Check

1 Sort these factors that affect development into the correct columns of the table:

climate   relief   colonialism   natural resources   debt   civil war   water supply   health and disease

Human factors	Physical factors

2 Why do you think health and disease are a human factor not a physical factor?

1. Human factors: colonialism, debt, civil war, health and disease. Physical factors: climate, relief, natural resources, water supply. 2. Even though health and disease are natural, they affect people. Also the effects of disease could be less if people did more to prevent them spreading.

9.4 International trade

International trade is the buying and selling of goods and services between countries.

Exports are goods and services that are sold to other countries.

Imports are goods and services that are bought from other countries.

The **balance of trade** is the difference between the total value of goods and services imported and the total value of goods and services exported.

A balance of trade **surplus** means a country has exported a greater value of goods and services than it has imported. The country has made money which it can invest.

A balance of trade **deficit** means a country has imported a greater value of goods and services than it has exported. The country has lost money. If this situation continues the country will need to borrow money.

> **Key Point**
> - International trade makes the countries of the world interdependent. Countries have become reliant on other countries, so that the success of one country affects the success of other countries.

Primary products are goods that are natural resources or raw materials. They have unstable prices, which means that their value can fall suddenly, and agricultural products are affected by pests, disease and poor weather.

Overdependence is when a country is dependent on one or a small number of exports. This makes the country vulnerable to problems with those exports or changes in the global market such as a fall in price or demand.

Trade should benefit all countries. Trade works best when a country trades a product that it can produce better than any other countries. As trade develops each country is able to specialise in the goods that it produces best, so that every country makes the most money possible and the world market has the highest possible quality of goods available.

Unfortunately trade doesn't always work like this. Many LEDCs have specialised in **primary products**. They export metal ores, minerals and agricultural products such as tea, coffee, cocoa and sugar which MEDCs cannot grow themselves. However, once an LEDC begins to import manufactured goods and services, which are more expensive, the LEDC can quickly fall into a **balance of trade deficit**.

The World Trade Organisation (WTO) was established in 1995. The aim of the WTO is to promote world trade and to reduce barriers to trade such as tariffs and quotas. People protest whenever the WTO meets because they argue that much international trade is damaging LEDCs and that more should be done to protect them from the negative effects of globalisation.

Barriers to trade are created by countries to control the amount of imports or exports. They are used to protect domestic industry from foreign competition. Tariffs are payments that have to be made for each item that is imported or exported. Quotas are limits on the number or amount of a product that can be imported or exported.

Fair trade

One method of helping LEDCs to make more money from their exports is through fair trade. Fair trade is a system where the producers of the raw materials for a product are given a fair price. They are also given long-term contracts, health and safety guarantees and extra help with education and housing. This is funded by increasing the cost of the finished product.

This works at a local level with individual farmers or a co-operative. But it also ensures that some of the problems of trading in a primary product are removed, which ultimately helps the country as a whole.

The most common fair trade products are tea, coffee, chocolate and fruit. Unfortunately, consumers in MEDCs are still not buying enough fair trade products to make a difference to more than a fraction of the producers in LEDCs. With increased awareness of fair trade products through charities like Oxfam, Traidcraft and Comic Relief, this situation is improving.

Progress Check

1. What is a trade surplus?
2. Which of these goods is a primary product? Iron ore, furniture, computers.
3. Why do people protest when there is a WTO meeting?
4. How can trade be made more fair?

1. A trade surplus is when a country exports more than it imports. 2. Iron ore. 3. Because the WTO promotes world trade, and some people think world trade is damaging the economies of some LEDCs. 4. By paying the producers of primary products more for their goods.

9.5 Transnational corporations

A transnational corporation (TNC) is a company that has interests in more than one country.

Profit is the amount of money that a company makes in a year.

World Rank	TNC	Profits (billion US$) 2001
1	Exxon Mobil	15.3
2	Citigroup	14.1
3	General Electric	13.7
4	Royal Dutch/Shell Group	10.9
5	Philip Morris Companies	8.6
6	BP	8.0
7	Pfizer	7.8
8	IBM	7.7
9	AT&T	7.7
10	Microsoft	7.3

Fig. 9.2 The world's largest TNCs by profit.

Key Point

The revenue of some TNCs is greater than the entire GDP of some LEDCs.

Usually the headquarters of TNCs and any research and development operations are found in MEDCs. Raw material extraction, processing, manufacture and assembly are found in LEDCs. TNCs will locate wherever they can make the most profit, and they choose LEDCs because wages are lower so the TNC can produce goods at less cost than in MEDCs. For example, the US-based TNC Nike has factories in Thailand.

Advantages and disadvantages of TNCs

Advantages of TNCs	Disadvantages of TNCs
Provide employment.	Jobs are often part-time or on short contracts.
Give a regular wage.	Labour is usually low paid.
People are trained and become skilled.	The highest skilled jobs are done by people from the country of origin of the TNC.
Increases the wealth of the surrounding area.	The profits from the TNC go back to the country of origin.
Brings new technology and facilities to the country.	The company could move out at any time.
Contributes to the development of infrastructure in the local area.	Standards of health and safety and environmental protection are often low.

Infrastructure includes the roads, railways, electricity, water supply and sanitation required for a business to operate successfully.

Fig. 9.3 Advantages and disadvantages of TNCs.

TNCs are now doing more to help the countries where they have interests, mainly as a result of pressure from consumers who are not prepared to buy goods from companies that exploit employees or countries. Many TNCs are leading the way in creating sustainable and energy efficient products. They are also involved in work with charities to improve the quality of life and standard of living for many people.

Progress Check

1 What is a TNC?

2 Why do TNCs build factories in LEDCs?

3 What happens to the profits that TNCs make from LEDCs?

4 Why are TNCs having to do more to help the countries where they are found?

1. A TNC is a company with interests in more than one country. 2. To take advantage of lower wages and new markets. 3. They go back to the country of origin of the TNC. 4. Mainly because of consumer pressure.

9.6 Aid

Key Point   Aid is help that is given by a country to another country.

Bilateral aid is aid that goes directly from one country to another.

Multilateral aid is aid that is given by an international organisation such as the United Nations.

Short-term aid is also known as emergency aid.

Short-term aid provides help to solve immediate problems following a natural disaster or war, for example. It includes food, water, tents, blankets and medical supplies.

Long-term aid funds projects that will have a lasting impact. It includes providing education and training, giving loans for projects such as dams or power stations, and providing a safe water supply.

Most countries give a proportion of their GNP to other countries as aid. The United Nations suggests that each country gives 0.7% of their GNP as aid.

In 2000 the UK gave $4.5 billion. However, this is the equivalent of only 0.31 per cent of the UK's GNP. The USA gave $9.6 billion, yet this is 0.1 per cent of its GNP. One of the most generous countries is Norway – it gave $1.26 billion, which is less than the UK or the USA, but is 0.92 per cent of its GNP.

The World Bank and the International Monetary Fund (IMF) are agencies of the United Nations which give aid. They were established after the Second World War to help countries develop and to encourage world trade. They provide **loans** to countries, which have to be paid back with interest. Frequently the type of aid they give is **conditional aid**.

Aid is also given by charities. These are known as non-governmental organisations (NGOs) because they are not connected to any national government. Charities involved with aid include Oxfam, the International Red Cross, Christian Aid, Cafod, WaterAid and Medecins Sans Frontières.

> Conditional aid is given with an agreement that the country receiving the aid will make certain changes, usually to its economy.

Progress Check

Complete the sentences using the words below.

1 Aid that is given from one country to another is known as _____ aid.

2 Aid that is given through an international organisation is known as _____ aid.

3 The United Nations organisation that handles aid donations is known as _____.

4 Charities that are not run by governments are known as _____.

the World Bank   multilateral   NGOs   bilateral

1. Bilateral. 2. Multilateral. 3. The World Bank. 4. NGOs.

9.7 Appropriate development

Aid sometimes fails to help a country to develop as much as it should. This can be for a number of reasons.

- **Corruption** in the country means the aid doesn't go to the people who are most in need.
- Countries spend more money **paying back the loans** for expensive projects than the money the projects make for the country.
- The **environment is damaged**, which costs money to put right.
- The aid that is provided is **too technical** for the skills of the population.
- The aid needs **expensive inputs** to keep it running each year.

For aid to be effective it must follow these conditions.

- It goes to the people who need it most.
- It provides value for money.
- It does not damage the environment.
- Local people are involved in the decision-making.
- The projects are small-scale.
- People have the skills to use the aid.
- The aid does not damage the culture of the people who receive it.
- The aid uses simple technology.
- The aid is sustainable – it meets the needs of the people without compromising their future needs.

Aid that meets these conditions is described as **appropriate aid**.

Simple technology which meets the skills of the people who will use it is known as **intermediate technology**.

Progress Check

Sort these items into two columns of generally appropriate or inappropriate types of aid.

nuclear power station   hand-powered water pump   dam
articulated lorry   bicycle   energy-efficient stove

Appropriate	Inappropriate

Appropriate: hand-powered water pump, bicycle, energy-efficient stove. Inappropriate: nuclear power station, dam, articulated lorry.

9.8 Debt

Key Point

Debt is the amount of money owed by countries to other countries or international organisations.

Globally the total amount of debt is over $300 billion.

Some countries, like the Philippines, have debt that is less than their GNP, so eventually they will be able to pay the debt off. For a country like Vietnam, the debt is more than its GNP, therefore it will be particularly hard to pay the debt off. Debt is paid back to the lending country with interest.

Jubilee 2000

Jubilee 2000 is an organisation that has been set up to campaign against debt. Since 1994 it has worked to encourage governments to cancel the debts owed to them by LEDCs. In 1999 the UK and the USA said they would cancel some of the debts owed to them on the condition that the countries would agree to the money being used to reduce poverty.

The UK is owed over $14.5 billion (£8 billion) by other countries. The UK receives over $121 million (£73.8 million) a year in debt repayments. It would cost Britain less than $123 million (£75 million) a year to cancel its international debts. This would cost Britain's 26 million taxpayers less than 4p a week or £2 a year, it is estimated.

Progress Check

1 Why are LEDCs in debt?

2 Why are some MEDCs unwilling to cancel their debts?

3 What could happen if debts were cancelled?

1. They have borrowed money to help pay for development projects. 2. Because MEDCs make money from the interest rates on the debts, and they are owed the money that they have lent. 3. LEDCs would have more money to spend on their own needs, such as healthcare and education.

Practice questions

The map shows the Human Development Index of most of the countries in the world.

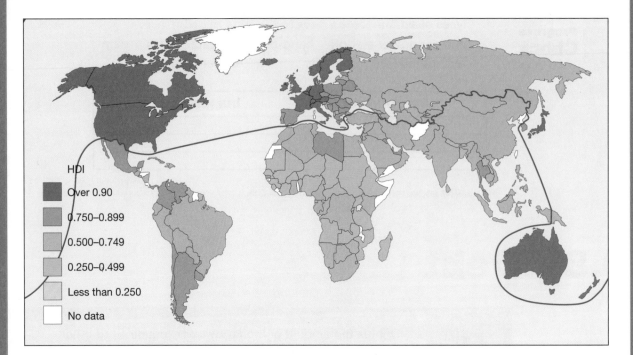

HDI

- Over 0.90
- 0.750–0.899
- 0.500–0.749
- 0.250–0.499
- Less than 0.250
- No data

1   Which three development indicators are used to measure the HDI?   **(3)**

2   What is the maximum and minimum HDI possible?   **(2)**

3   Where are most countries with an HDI of less than 0.500 found?   **(1)**

4   Describe the distribution of countries with an HDI of over 0.90.   **(3)**

5   Give three reasons why some countries are more developed than others.   **(6)**

10 Environmental and resource issues

The topics covered in this chapter are:

● **Sustainable development**
● **Energy sources and alternative energy**
● **Land, water and air**
● **Waste and recycling**

After studying this topic you should be able to:

● describe sustainable development
● understand the world's increasing demand for energy
● describe and explain the issues surrounding wind power
● identify the causes and consequences of soil erosion
● account for the inequalities in global supplies of water
● explain global warming
● argue in favour of recycling.

10.1 Sustainable development

Key Point — Sustainable development is development that meets the needs of the present generation without compromising the ability of future generations to meet their needs.

Sustainable development concerns the relationship between people and the environment. People must take care of the environment if the human race is to continue to develop, so that standards of living and quality of life increase for all.

Golden rules of sustainable development

Sustainable development operates in the long term. It requires careful planning and management and it can involve making sacrifices in the present to safeguard future prosperity. Sometimes people in authority are unwilling to engage in sustainable development because they will be making unpopular decisions with no obvious benefit during their time in office.

Replacement and recycling
● Use resources in a way that does not damage the environment.

> If a country is in debt, present citizens are paying for money that previous citizens have benefited from.

- Make sure that resources are being used as efficiently as possible with a minimum of waste.
- Replace resources when they have been used.
- Recycle resources whenever possible.

Development without debt

- Develop services and industry without taking out loans that cannot be paid back.
- Realise that debt restricts the provision of vital services such as healthcare and education. It also limits a country's potential to develop further.

Appropriate technology

- Acquire technology that the country can afford, that doesn't damage the environment and that its citizens are able to use and repair independently from other countries.
- Realise that inappropriate technology can be too expensive and lead to debt, and it can damage the environment and lead to dependency on other countries.

Earth Summit on Environment and Development – Rio de Janeiro 1992

As a response to the need for sustainable development, the leaders of 153 nations met in Rio de Janeiro, Brazil, in 1992. It was the first time the majority of the world's countries had met to discuss the global environment and sustainable development. It was recognised that many environmental problems do not respect national boundaries and that countries have to work together in order to solve them.

The Earth Summit produced an agreement known as 'Agenda 21', a blueprint for sustainable development for the 21st century. Each country produced an action plan which they are now meant to be following to achieve sustainable development.

Biodiversity

As well as recognising the importance of sustainable development, Agenda 21 also highlights the importance of maintaining biodiversity.

Biodiversity is the rich variety of life on Earth. Agenda 21 tells us that it is our responsibility to protect the 1.7 million species that exist as a result of 3000 million years of evolution.

Sustainable development not only promotes the well-being of the human race, it respects all life on the planet.

Progress Check

1 What is sustainable development?
2 Why does sustainable development require international cooperation?
3 What is biodiversity?

1. Sustainable development is development that meets the needs of the present generation without compromising the ability of future generations to meet their needs. 2. Many environmental problems do not respect national boundaries so countries have to work together in order to solve them. 3. The rich variety of life on Earth.

10.2 Energy sources

Biomass fuels are traditional sources of energy such as firewood, crop waste, peat and dung.

Energy is anything that can be used to provide power.

Fuel is something that is burned to release energy in the form of heat, which can be transformed into power.

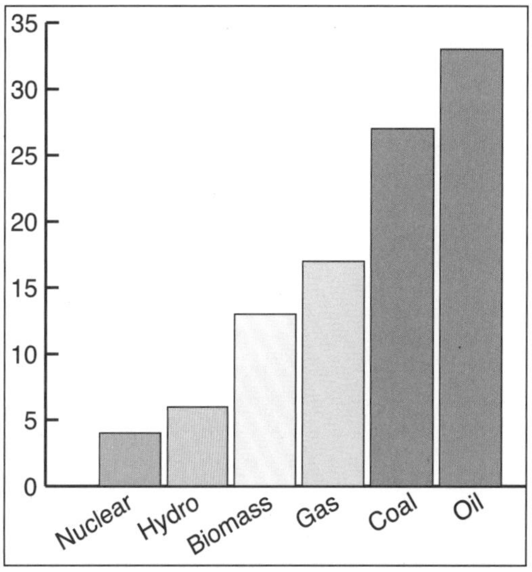

Fig. 10.1 Sources of world energy.

Fossil fuels

> **Key Point**
>
> The world gets over 75 per cent of its energy from fossil fuels.

Fossil fuels are coal, oil and natural gas. They are natural resources which have formed over millions of years from organic matter – dead plants and creatures.

Fossil fuels are a **non-renewable** source of energy. This means that once they have been used they cannot be replaced. It has been estimated that global coal reserves will last for 200–400 years, natural gas for 120 years and oil for 50 years.

Reserves of fossil fuels are not evenly distributed across the world.

UK coal reserves should last for another 300 years, oil and gas for another 40 years.

China and the USA account for over half of the world's supplies of coal. Other countries with large coal reserves include India, South Africa, Australia, Russia and Poland. Coal used to be extracted by digging tunnels underground, but today it is more efficient and safer to dig coal from the surface downwards in a system known as open cast mining.

Russia and the USA produce over half the world's supplies of natural gas. Canada, the UK, the Netherlands, Algeria and Indonesia are also major producers of natural gas.

Much of the world's oil is produced by the countries of OPEC, the Organisation of Petroleum Exporting Countries. Members of OPEC are Algeria, Ecuador, Gabon, Indonesia, Iran, Iraq, Kuwait, Libya, Nigeria, Qatar, Saudi Arabia, the United Arab Emirates and Venezuela. OPEC accounts for more than 25 per cent of the world's oil supplies. Other oil producing countries are the USA at 11 per cent, Russia at 9 per cent, Mexico, China and the UK.

Problems of fossil fuels

Using fossil fuels damages the environment in a number of ways:
- Open cast mining uses up large areas of the countryside and causes noise and dust.
- Oil spills at sea cause oil slicks that kill sea life and birds.
- Burning fossil fuels releases chemicals that cause acid rain, smog and global warming.

Eventually supplies of fossil fuels will run out, so people have to find alternative sources of energy before this happens.

The amount of energy that the world consumes is growing at an increasing rate. In 1895 world energy consumption was the equivalent of 500 million tonnes of oil a year. By 1955 this had increased to over 2 billion tonnes, in 1995 the energy use was over 8 billion tonnes and it currently stands at over 10 billion tonnes. It has been predicted that this will double to over 20 billion tonnes by 2050.

The largest consumer of energy is the USA, which uses the equivalent of 7.87 million tonnes of oil per person a year. The UK consumes the equivalent of 3.69 million tonnes of oil per person a year.

MEDCs consume more energy than LEDCs. 79 per cent of the world's population live in LEDCs but they consume only 30 per cent of the world's energy. However, this situation is changing as industry declines and environmental protection increases in MEDCs, and industrialisation continues in LEDCs.

Progress Check

1 Which of these is not a fossil fuel?

   coal   gas   uranium   oil

2 Which of these countries is not a member of OPEC?

   UK   Kuwait   Iraq   Algeria

3 Which of these problems is not caused by burning fossil fuels?

   global warming   acid rain   smog   the hole in the ozone layer

1. Uranium. 2. UK. 3. The hole in the ozone layer.

10.3 Alternative energy

Alternative energy is any source of power that is not a fossil fuel. Most alternative energy is renewable.

Key Point
The world gains approximately 25 per cent of its energy from alternative energy sources.

Renewable energy is energy that will not run out. This includes resources that can be used again and again such as tidal, geothermal, wind, wave or solar power, or resources that can be replaced once they have been used such as wood for burning or alcohol fuel made from sugar cane.

Hydroelectric power (HEP)

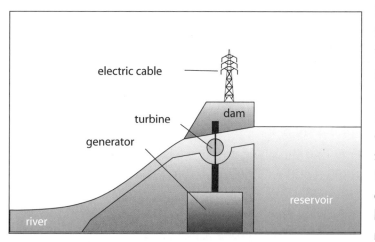

Fig. 10.3 Generating electricity by HEP.

HEP is electricity that is generated from fast flowing water. The water passes through turbines which spin, driving generators which produce electricity.

HEP is relatively expensive to develop because most HEP schemes involve constructing large dams so that a constant supply of water at sufficient pressure can be created to drive the turbines. However, once the dams have been built HEP is a low-cost source of energy which is renewable, as long as it rains.

Fig. 10.4 Countries which generate a significant proportion of their electricity from HEP.

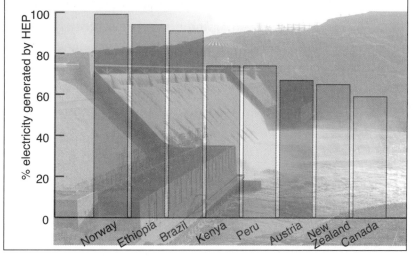

There are problems with HEP:
- The reservoirs behind the dams flood land; wildlife habitats are destroyed, farmland is lost forever and people have to be relocated.
- The dams also fill up with silt transported by rivers. This prevents the silt reaching farmland downstream and fertilising it, and eventually will clog up the reservoir unless it is removed.
- The high cost of dams has put some LEDCs into debt.
- There is a danger of dams collapsing, particularly if they are built in earthquake zones.

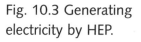

The UK generates 2 per cent of its electricity from HEP.

In China the world's largest dam is being built in the Three Gorges region of the Yangtse river. Work began in 1993 and it is expected to be completed in 2009. It will cost as much as $17 billion to build. The dam will be 2 km long and over 100 m high, and the reservoir will stretch for 600 km behind the dam. The dam will generate 18 000 megawatts of electricity. 1.3 million people will have to be moved from their homes because of the flooding, including 320 villages and 140 towns. 40,000 hectares of farmland will be lost, as will the outstandingly beautiful Three Gorges section of the river. Rare species are threatened by the dam, including freshwater dolphins, alligators, tigers and pandas.

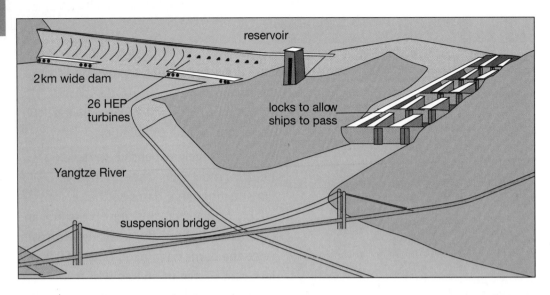

reservoir

2km wide dam

26 HEP turbines

locks to allow ships to pass

Yangtze River

suspension bridge

Fig. 10.5 The Three Gorges Dam.

Wind power

Fig. 10.6 Wind turbines.

Wind power is electricity generated using wind turbines.

Wind power can only be generated in places with a lot of wind, such as coastal locations and high land.

Like HEP, wind turbines are expensive to construct but relatively cheap to run.

Wind turbines take up little land, which can still be used for farming, as livestock can graze in the same field.

The largest wind farm in the world is at Altamont Pass in California, with 7000 wind turbines. The state of California has a total of 16 000 wind turbines, enough to power San Francisco.

The UK has approximately 550 wind turbines, enough to power 400 000 homes. The largest wind farm is in Camelford in Cornwall, providing sufficient electricity to power 3000 homes. The government has set up a goal of producing 10 per cent of the UK's electricity from wind energy by 2025. Currently the UK generates less than 1 per cent of its electricity from wind.

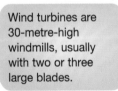

Wind turbines are 30-metre-high windmills, usually with two or three large blades.

7000 wind turbines are required to produce the same amount of electricity as an average fossil fuel power station.

Problems with wind turbines
- They are expensive to build.
- Some people say they are ugly and spoil the landscape.
- Some people claim they are noisy and interfere with television reception.
- They will not work if there is not enough wind.

Energy efficiency

To complement efforts to find alternative energy resources, people are being encouraged to become more energy efficient. Not only does this provides savings for homes and businesses, it also reduces the amount of fossil fuels that are being burnt. This will help the fossil fuels to last longer,

Fig. 10.8 Energy
Efficiency logo.

Energy Efficiency is
an Energy Saving
Trust initiative backed
by the Government.

and less pollution such as acid rain and emissions causing global warming
will occur.

Energy efficient methods include:

- fitting insulation
- using low energy lightbulbs
- taking a shower not a bath to save hot water
- turning off electrical items completely instead of leaving
  them on standby
- boiling only enough water that you need in a kettle
- putting lids on pans when you cook
- using public transport
- sharing car journeys.

Progress Check

True or false?

1 The world generates 10 per cent of its electricity from alternative energy sources.

2 HEP does not damage the environment.

3 The UK generates 2 per cent of its electricity from HEP.

4 7000 wind turbines can generate as much electricity as one fossil fuel power
station.

5 1 million homes are powered by wind turbines in the UK.

1. False – the answer is 25 per cent. 2. False – the lakes that build up behind HEP dams can destroy
habitats. 3. True. 4. True. 5. False – the answer is 400 000.

10.4 Land

Soil erosion

Key Point

**Soil is one of our most important resources – without it we
would not be able to produce any food.**

It takes an average of
1000 years to form
1 cm of soil, therefore
it is important to
protect soil.

Some 75 million tonnes of soil are lost every year due to soil erosion. The
soil is either blown away by wind or washed away by rain. 1 billion people
live in areas at risk from soil erosion.

Soil erosion is made worse by removing vegetation. Plants protect soil by
intercepting rain before it reaches the ground and holding the soil surface
together with roots. Removing plants exposes soil to the full force of wind
and rain. The problem is made worse as the gradient of a slope increases.

Main causes of soil loss

- **Overgrazing** – if too many animals are allowed to graze in an area,
  the vegetation can be lost, and once the soil has been eroded it will
  not return.

- **Up and down ploughing** – if farmers plough slopes from top to bottom, the furrows that are created encourage rainwater to flow downhill, increasing the amount of soil that is eroded.
- **Deforestation** – cutting down trees for farming, settlement or industry exposes the soil and can create huge amounts of soil erosion.
- **Soil exhaustion** – fertile soil contains nutrients and minerals that hold the soil together; if a soil becomes infertile due to overcultivation it erodes more easily.

Solutions to the problem of soil erosion

- **Fencing** – to control the number of animals grazing in an area.
- **Contour ploughing** – if farmers plough along a slope, the furrows create mini-dams, preventing the downward movement of soil.
- **Terracing** – building fields in a series of steps down a slope, preventing water from running downhill and causing soil erosion.
- **Tree planting** – replacing trees that have been lost to deforestation.
- **Small dams** – to prevent gullies getting bigger.
- **Placing stones along contours** – this low-tech approach is very effective in reducing soil erosion, as soil is trapped by the stones and the flow of water is disrupted.

Causes	Solutions
Overgrazing	Fencing
Up and down ploughing	Contour ploughing
Deforestation	Tree planting
Soil exhaustion	Terracing

Fig. 10.9 Causes and solutions of soil erosion.

Progress Check

1 How much soil is eroded each year worldwide?
2 Why is soil so important?
3 How do plants help to reduce soil erosion?

1. 75 million tonnes. 2. Without soil we would not be able to grow enough food. 3. Plants reduce soil erosion by intercepting rain, providing shelter from wind, adding new organic matter and holding the soil together with their roots.

10.5 Water

Water is essential for human life. We need it for drinking, cooking, washing, farming and industry. Some 60 to 70 per cent of the human body is water. Without water we would only live for three to six days.

However, less than 0.01 per cent of the world's water is fresh water available for drinking.

> **Key Point**
>
> ○ There are vast inequalities in access to clean water across
> ○ the world.
> ○

Facts about world water

- 2 billion people live in places that have a shortage of water.
- 1 billion people do not have access to safe drinking water.
- 10 million people die every year from diseases spread in dirty water.
- Many hours are spent by people in LEDCs collecting water daily. This is time that could be spent in education, work or leisure.
- Over 50 per cent of the world's population do not have access to adequate sanitation. Sanitation is the hygienic removal of human waste.

> The number of people who suffer from a shortage of water is expected to increase, and the United Nations has predicted that by 2025 as many as 4 billion people will have a severe shortage of water. This is mainly due to population increase.

A number of international organisations and charities are working to provide more people with clean water supplies. These include WaterAid, Global Water, Oxfam, Cafod, Christian Aid and the United Nations.

For example, in Silchari, a village in Bangladesh, it now takes children five minutes to collect water from a tap that has been connected to a water supply underground. Previously, the children had to walk for an hour with a heavy water container. People in the village are no longer becoming sick from drinking unclean water.

The UK's water supplies

In the UK we have plenty of water.

There are four main sources of water supply in the UK:

- **Rivers** – these provide most of the UK's drinking water. The water is usually stored in artificial reservoirs before it is cleaned and piped to people's homes.
- **Wells** – rocks underground that are able to store water are known as **aquifers**. They give a pure source of water because it is filtered as it passes through the rock. The water is reached by digging wells and drilling bore holes into the aquifer.

> Impermeable rock is rock that does not let water pass through it.

- **Springs** – where water bubbles to the ground surface. They are found when an aquifer lies on top of impermeable rock. Once an aquifer has been filled with water any excess water flows out of the ground as a spring.
- **Reservoirs** – these are built in upland areas to collect water that would otherwise be carried by rivers to the sea. The water is then transferred via pipes or rivers to places that need it.

Water shortages

It is not unusual for the UK to suffer from water shortages in the summer, despite the high levels of rainfall. One reason is that most rain falls in the north and west of the UK and the highest densities of population are found in the south and east. Water transfer schemes do exist, such as the Kielder reservoir in Northumberland that supplies water to the north-east of the UK. However, during long, dry summers people are encouraged to use water conservation techniques.

Water conservation techniques

- Take a shower not a bath.
- Don't leave the tap running when you brush your teeth.
- Don't wash your car.
- Don't use a hose to water the garden.
- Put a device called a hippo in your toilet cistern to reduce the amount of water that is flushed.

In extreme droughts, such as the drought of 1976, people were forced to use standpipes. Water supplies to people's homes were switched off and they had to use a tap in the street.

Progress Check

Complete the sentences below.

1 The number of people in the world without access to safe water is

_____.

2 An organisation that is working to provide clean water supplies is

_____.

3 The UK gets most of its water from _____.

4 A device that you put in your toilet cistern to save water is known as a

_____.

1. 1 billion. 2. WaterAid, Global Water, Oxfam, Cafod, Christian Aid or the United Nations. 3. Rivers. 4. Hippo.

10.6 Air

The atmosphere

The Earth's atmosphere is 78 per cent nitrogen and 21 per cent oxygen. The remaining 1 per cent is mainly argon, with some water vapour, carbon dioxide and methane.

99 per cent of the Earth's atmosphere is found between the Earth's surface and 30 km above us. Most of our weather occurs between the surface and 10 km above us. The **ozone layer** is between 30 and 40 km above the Earth.

The weight of the atmosphere pressing down on us is known as **atmospheric pressure**. At sea level average atmospheric pressure is 1013 millibars.

Air pollution

Key Point

Since the Industrial Revolution in the middle of the 18th century the atmosphere has been increasingly polluted by chemicals and gases.

One of the most worrying consequences of atmospheric pollution is global warming. This is caused by pollutants increasing the greenhouse effect.

The greenhouse effect

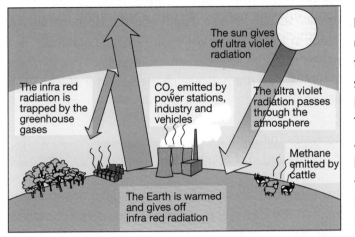

Fig. 10.10 The greenhouse effect.

Radiation from the sun is in the form of ultraviolet radiation. It is able to pass through the Earth's atmosphere and heat up the surface of the Earth. As the surface of the Earth is heated it gives off infrared radiation. This is not able to pass through the Earth's atmosphere, so it is trapped in the lower layers of the atmosphere and the air is warmed. Without the greenhouse effect no heat would be trapped and conditions would be too cold for life to exist.

The gases in the atmosphere that trap the infrared radiation are mainly carbon dioxide and methane.

Carbon dioxide is produced when trees or fossil fuels are burnt. Methane is produced by bogs and the digestion process of most animals, especially cattle.

The USA is responsible for 30 per cent of the world's carbon dioxide emissions, while the UK is responsible for 6 per cent.

As countries develop, large amounts of carbon dioxide are released into the atmosphere. In addition, deforestation means that fewer trees absorb less carbon dioxide. Most scientists now agree that increasing carbon dioxide in the atmosphere is causing more infrared radiation to be trapped and average temperatures are going up.

Between 1900 and 1999 the world emitted an estimated 250 billion tonnes of carbon dioxide by burning fossil fuels. The 20 countries that emitted the most carbon dioxide during this time were responsible for 200 billion tonnes of that total. The top five countries were the USA, Russia, Germany, China and the UK.

Effects of global warming

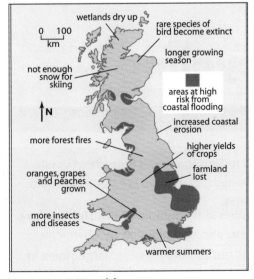

Fig. 10.11 Possible impacts of global warming on the UK.

Global warming will have two catastrophic effects.

The migration of the earth's climatic zones towards the North and South Poles

- In Russia and Canada previously frozen northern wastelands will be able to support agriculture.
- In North America and Eastern Europe grain harvests will decline.
- In Africa and South America forests will be replaced by deserts as the continents become warmer and drier.
- The UK could have a more Mediterranean climate able to support a thriving wine, olive and citrus fruit industry.

Sea level rises

- Sea levels will rise because the extra heat will cause the sea to expand. This could cause levels to rise between 0.25 and 1.5 metres.

Some people fear that poisonous creatures and tropical diseases will also move towards the North and South Poles.

- The polar ice caps and some glaciers will melt, and the extra water released could cause sea levels to rise by a further 5 metres.
- Low-lying countries such as Bangladesh, Egypt and the Netherlands will be flooded, and islands in the Pacific and Indian Oceans containing unique and rare species could be lost forever.
- The coastline of the UK will be dramatically changed and many coastal towns and cities will be flooded.

Attempts to limit global warming

Global conferences have produced agreements to reduce global warming. In the 1992 Earth Summit in Rio de Janeiro, countries agreed to cut carbon dioxide levels by the year 2000 to the levels that they were in 1990. At the climate change conference in Kyoto in 1997, countries agreed to cut emissions by 5.2 per cent of 1990 levels by 2012.

Governments have acted to control carbon dioxide in their countries. This includes passing laws to ensure that industry is not releasing excess emissions, increasing taxes on fossil fuels, encouraging citizens to be more energy efficient and researching alternative energy sources.

Progress Check

1 Name two greenhouse gases.
2 Why are there more greenhouse gases in the atmosphere than there were 200 years ago?
3 What will be the likely effect of global warming on the UK?
4 How can countries prevent global warming from happening?

1. Carbon dioxide, methane. 2. As the countries of the world have developed, carbon dioxide has been released when trees and fossil fuels have been burnt. Also, with fewer trees, less carbon dioxide is being absorbed. 3. The coast of the UK will change, settlements will be flooded, new crops can be grown, it might get warmer, and the UK could suffer from new pests and diseases. 4. By encouraging people to be energy efficient, using alternative energy sources and passing laws controlling greenhouse gas emissions.

10.7 Waste and recycling

Waste

Key Point
The UK produces about 25 million tonnes of household waste a year, the equivalent of the weight of a small car per household, or 350 kg of waste per person.

Some 83 per cent of the UK's waste is put in **landfill sites**, large holes in the ground which are usually former quarries or gravel pits. The landfill sites are lined with clay to prevent the seepage of toxic chemicals. They are covered over when they are full and developed for agriculture, housing or industry.

	Percentage of waste
Paper and card	33
Food waste	20
Plastic	11
Other	10
Glass	9
Dust	7
Steel cans	6
Textiles	2
Aluminium	2

Fig. 10.12 An average household's rubbish.

The problem is that landfill sites are filling up in the UK, and locations for new ones are running out. People do not want a landfill site near them because of the noise from waste lorries, pests such as rats and sea gulls, smells, windblown waste and the risk of chemicals seeping into the water supply.

Landfill sites need to be constructed with a system to collect and burn off the methane that is produced as the waste decomposes. The methane can be used to generate electricity. If it was not collected and burned, landfill sites would contribute to global warming and they could explode!

Nine per cent of the UK's waste is incinerated, which means that it is burned in huge furnaces. This can cause pollution, particularly of toxic gases as plastics are burned. However, some incinerators use the heat that is produced to generate electricity.

Recycling

Recycling is the alternative to incineration or landfill. The UK recycles 8 per cent of its waste, but we could recycle up to 80 per cent.

Recycling saves natural resources – it takes less energy and produces less pollution than making the product from raw materials. For example, glass takes 20 per cent less energy to recycle and causes 20 per cent less pollution, while aluminium takes 95 per cent less energy to recycle and causes 99 per cent less pollution.

It takes 25 plastic drinks bottles to make one fleece jacket.

MEDCs are more wasteful than LEDCs. LEDCs are better at recycling, as everything is more precious. Many shanty towns are constructed from materials that wealthier people have thrown away. In LEDCs some people make a living by sorting through rubbish in tips and identifying material that can be recycled or reused. In Nairobi, people at Kirkumba market sell woks made from oil drums, lamps made from tin cans and axe heads made from hinges.

The UK is behind other countries in recycling its waste. The USA recycles 13 per cent of its waste and Japan recycles 33 per cent.

The UK government has set targets for local authorities that they must recycle 33 per cent of their waste by 2015 and reduce the amount of waste that goes in landfill sites by 65 per cent by 2020.

A final method of reducing waste and protecting resources is to reduce the amount of packaging that is used. One quarter of waste in UK is from packaging, the equivalent of 5 million tonnes in weight. The European Union has recently introduced a rule that countries must recycle 60 per cent of their packaging waste and incinerate 30 per cent to generate electricity.

Progress Check

1 Match the waste product with the recycled alternative.

Waste product	Recycled alternative
plastic bottles	axe head
oil drum	lamp
tin can	wok
hinge	fleece jacket

2 Why is recycling better than making products from new each time?

3 How much of the UK's waste could be recycled?

1. Plastic bottles = fleece jacket, oil drum = wok, hinge = axe head, tin can = lamp. 2. Recycling is cheaper and more energy efficient than making a product from new, it prevents natural resources from being wasted unnecessarily and it stops landfill sites from being used up. 3. 80 per cent.

Practice questions

The photographs show some of the world's endangered species. An endangered species is a creature that is likely to become extinct.

1	What is biodiversity?	(1)
2	What is wrong with losing biodiversity?	(3)
3	Describe three ways that people's use of resources can destroy wildlife habitats.	(3)
4	How can people's use of resources be managed to conserve biodiversity?	(3)

11 Australia

The topics covered in this chapter are:

- Physical geography
- Population and settlement
- Development
- Agriculture and industry
- The Outback
- Sydney

After studying this topic you should be able to:

- describe the physical landscape, climate and vegetation of Australia
- explain the population distribution in Australia
- describe the quality of life, and inequalities, in Australia
- understand Australian agriculture
- describe Australian industry
- appreciate the differences between rural and urban areas in Australia.

11.1 Physical geography

Australia is the world's largest island, and is 32 times larger than the UK.

 Key Point

Australia's size results in a huge variety of landscapes including deserts, grasslands, rainforests, mountains, plains and a spectacular coastline.

It would take you about two weeks to drive from the east coast to the west coast of Australia.

Total land area	7 682 300 km²
Distance from north to south	3680 km
Distance from east to west	4000 km

Physical landscape

Australia's landscape can be divided into three areas:

- **The Western Plateau** – a vast, flat area of ancient rocks, including the Hamersley Mountains.
- **The Central Lowlands** – a lowland area which used to be a sea. This is where one of Australia's most spectacular landforms, Uluru (Ayer's Rock), is found.
- **The Eastern Highlands** – a chain of mountains running along Australia's east coast. These mountains include the Great Dividing Range, and the Australian Alps.

Climate

Rainfall

After Antarctica, Australia is the world's driest continent.

The centre of Australia has a desert climate, receiving less than 250 mm of rainfall per year. The areas to the north and east of the desert are wet during the summer, but dry during the winter. The areas that receive most rainfall are around the north and east coasts. The north coast has a tropical monsoon climate, which results in some places receiving over 2000 mm of rainfall a year.

Temperature

Australia is in the southern hemisphere, which means the hottest temperatures are in December, and the coolest temperatures are in June. The hottest areas are in the north of the country, because they are closest to the equator. Temperatures in desert areas can reach 50°C in the summer.

Vegetation

The huge variations in Australia's climate result in several different types of ecosystem:

- **Desert** – the hot, dry deserts at the centre of Australia contain mainly scattered grasses. The grasses have adapted to the climate by growing very long roots.
- **Tropical grassland** – the area known as the Bush contains grasses and scattered Eucalyptus trees.
- **Tropical rainforest** – the heavy rainfall and high temperatures of the northern coast result in dense tropical rainforests.

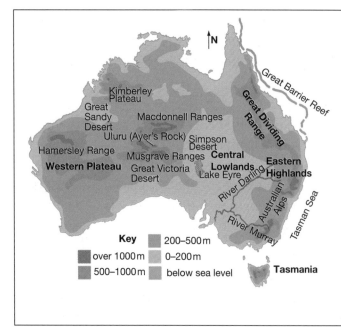

Fig. 11.1 Physical map of Australia.

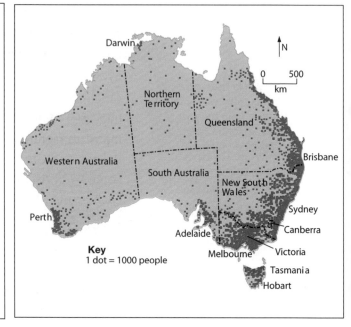

Fig. 11.2 Population distribution.

Progress Check

Match the physical regions below with the correct description.

Central Lowlands   Western Plateau   Eastern Highlands

1 A vast, flat area of ancient rocks.
2 A lowland area which used to be a sea.
3 A chain of mountains including the Australian Alps.

1. Western Plateau. 2. Central Lowlands. 3. Eastern Highlands.

11.2 Population and settlement

Population distribution

Key Point

Australia has a population of 19.5 million people, who are spread out very unevenly across the country.

Few people live in the central part of Australia because of the harsh desert climate. The conditions make it a difficult place to live and work.

Most people live in settlements along the east and south-east coasts. Coastal locations have a more pleasant climate. The most popular places to live are the cities of Sydney, Melbourne, Adelaide and Brisbane. These cities grew up around natural harbours, which are very important for trade with other countries. Canberra, the capital of Australia, is the only inland city.

Immigrants

Almost all Australians are immigrants, or descended from immigrants. European people began migrating to Australia following the founding of Sydney, by Captain Cook, in 1788.

Originally Britain sent criminals to Australia. Later, many British people migrated to Australia in search of a better life. After the Second World War, many immigrants moved to Australia from Europe. The largest groups were Italians and Greeks. Most recently, the largest group of immigrants have come from Asian countries, such as Vietnam, the Philippines and Malaysia. Each group of immigrants have brought with them elements of their own culture and enriched the Australian way of life.

Aboriginal people

The original inhabitants of Australia are called Aborigines. Aboriginal people are thought to have migrated from south-east Asia around 50 000 years ago when sea levels were much lower.

When the British immigrants first arrived there were around 750 000 Aborigines. Many of them died as a result of diseases introduced by the

> Traditionally Aborigines lived off the land as hunters and gatherers.

British, and because the British settlers treated them very badly. Today there are around 400 000 Aborigines living in Australia. Although most now live in towns and cities, many still live in remote areas in the **Bush**.

Progress Check

Cross out the incorrect words in the sentences below.
1 The population of Australia is evenly/unevenly distributed.
2 Most people live in coastal/desert locations.
3 The capital of Australia is Canberra/Sydney.
4 The most recent immigrants to Australia are from Europe/Asia.
5 The original inhabitants of Australia were Aborigines/British.

Incorrect words: 1. evenly. 2. desert. 3. Sydney. 4. Europe. 5. British.

11.3 Development

Quality of life

Key Point

The quality of life in Australia can be measured using a range of indicators.

The table below compares the indicators for Australia with those for the UK.

> The United Nations ranks Australia as the seventh most developed country in the world.

Australia	Indicator	UK
0.938	Human Development Index	0.918
$27 000	GDP per capita	$20 730
0.96%	Population growth rate	0.1%
77 male, 83 female	Life expectancy	75 male, 79 female
5%	Percentage working in agriculture	2%
22%	Percentage working in industry	29%
73%	Percentage working in services	69%
100%	Literacy	99%
13	Birth rate	13
7	Death rate	11
5	Infant mortality rate	6
519	Number of TV sets per 1000 people	612

Fig. 11.3 Key comparative indicators between the UK and Australia.

Inequalities

Although Australia is a relatively wealthy nation, not everybody has a high standard of living. Over 800 000 people live below the official **poverty line**. The most disadvantaged group of Australians are **Aboriginal** people.

- The unemployment rate for Aborigines is three times the national average.
- The average salary for Aborigines is 35 per cent less than the national average.
- Fewer than a third of Aboriginal people own their own homes.
- Life expectancy for Aborigines is 20 years lower than the national average.
- Only 12 per cent of Aborigines go to university. The national rate is 36 per cent.

Aborigines have a lower quality of life for a number of reasons. For many years after the arrival of European settlers they were mistreated and denied basic human rights. During the 1950s and 1960s it was government policy to end the traditional Aboriginal lifestyle and Aboriginal children were taken from their parents to be raised in children's homes. Aboriginal culture was considered worthless. It was not until 1967 that Aborigines were recognised as Australian citizens. Although many Aboriginal people now live comfortable lives, as a group they lag behind other Australians.

Progress Check

True or false?

1 Australians live longer that British people.

2 British people are more wealthy than Australians.

3 Australians have fewer TV sets than the British.

4 The average life expectancy for Aborigines is 20 years less than for white Australians.

5 Aborigines earn more than white Australians.

1. True. 2. False. 3. True. 4. True. 5. False.

11.4 Agriculture

Key Point

Farming has been a very important industry in Australia since the arrival of the first settlers. Today, agricultural produce, including wool, beef, wheat, fruit and wine, earn over a third of Australia's income from exports.

Types of farming

The largest Australian sheep farms are bigger than UK counties.

Sheep farms cover vast areas, especially in the drier parts of New South Wales and Western Australia. Merino sheep, which produce high-quality wool, were brought to Australia from South Africa in the 1800s. Money earned from exporting wool earned much of Australia's early wealth, helping to develop its economy. Australia is still the world's largest exporter of wool, producing 25 per cent of the global total.

The most important area for **beef farming** is the northern state of Queensland. Cattle are allowed to graze freely until it is time for them to go to market. Much of Australia's beef is exported to the USA and Japan.

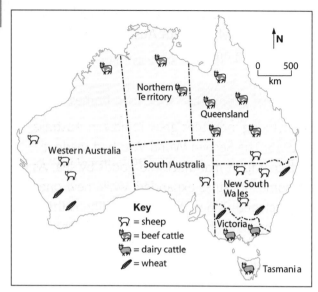

Dairy cattle are farmed in the southern states of Victoria and Tasmania, where the grass is better quality. These farms are located closer to main cities where fresh milk is needed.

Wheat is grown all over Australia, especially in the south-east and south-west. Technology has been used to increase the area that can be farmed. Poor soils have been improved with fertiliser, and crops are watered using irrigation systems. The main customers for Australia's wheat are China, Egypt and the USA.

Fig. 11.4 Agriculture in Australia.

Progress Check

1 What popular breed of sheep in Australia produces high-quality wool?
2 What percentage of the world's wool is produced in Australia?
3 Which are the most important areas for sheep farming in Australia?
4 Which are the most important areas for dairy farming in Australia?
5 Name two countries that are major importers of Australian wheat.

1. Merino. 2. 25 per cent. 3. New South Wales and Western Australia. 4. Victoria and Tasmania. 5. China, Egypt, USA.

11.5 Industry

Resources

Key Point

Australia is rich in mineral resources, which it exports all over the world.

Australia has large reserves of metal ores, like bauxite, iron ore, copper and nickel. It has energy resources of coal, oil, gas and uranium. It also has precious metals and gemstones, including gold and diamonds. Money earned from exports has made Australia one of the world's wealthiest countries.

Mining

Mining takes place in many areas of the country, but is most important in Western Australia. This province is home to iron ore mines in the Pilbarra region, bauxite (aluminium ore) mines around Perth, diamond mines in the

Kimberley region and gold mines near Kalgoorlie. In addition, coal mines and oil wells are found in Queensland, while South Australia and Northern Territory are important uranium mining areas.

Manufacturing

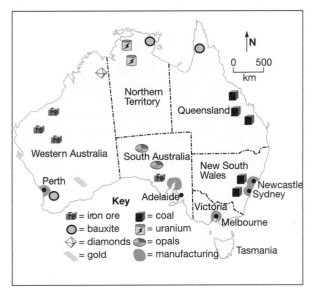

Manufacturing industries grew rapidly in Australia after 1945. The Second World War had made it difficult to import manufactured goods by sea. As a result, some industries expanded, while new ones were developed. Today, metal production is the most important industry, followed by food processing and the manufacture of machinery. Manufacturing is concentrated around the cities of Sydney, Newcastle, Melbourne and Adelaide.

Fig. 11.5 Mining and manufacturing in Australia.

Progress Check

Match the type of mining with the correct area.

1 Iron ore mining.

2 Bauxite mining.

3 Diamond mining.

4 Coal mining.

5 Uranium mining.

Queensland   Pilbarra   Northern Territory   Perth   Kimberley

1. Pilbarra. 2. Perth. 3. Kimberley. 4. Queensland. 5. Northern Territory.

11.6 The outback

Key Point

The outback is the interior part of Australia, away from the coast.

Coober Pedy

Coober Pedy gets its name from the Aboriginal words, 'Kupa Piti'. This translates as 'white man's hole in the ground'.

Few people live in the outback, but the unusual town of Coober Pedy is home to 2500 people. Coober Pedy is an isolated settlement, the nearest large town being Alice Springs, 690 km to the north. The closest city is Adelaide, 850 km to the south.

The harsh desert climate has resulted in an unusual way of living for the people of Coober Pedy. Most of the population live in underground homes, or caves, called 'dugouts', to avoid the intense heat. The dugouts are kept at a comfortable 26°C by ventilation holes drilled through the rock.

Environment

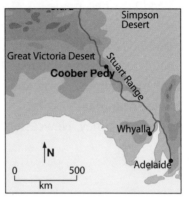

Coober Pedy lies at the southern end of the Stuart Mountain Range. To the west is the Great Victorian Desert. Coober Pedy has one of the most extreme climates in Australia. The average annual rainfall is only 157 mm. During the day it can be extremely hot, even reaching 50°C. At night the temperature can drop to freezing. Dust storms can occur when it is windy. Little vegetation is able to survive in these conditions.

Fig. 11.6 Location of Coober Pedy.

Economy

In the 1960s European migrants came to Coober Pedy seeking their fortune and today there are people from 53 different countries living in the town.

A favourite activity is 'noodling' – searching through rubble looking for pieces of opal missed by miners.

Most people in Coober Pedy are involved in opal mining or tourism.

Opals are gemstones used to make jewellery. The sandstone rock around Coober Pedy contains the valuable stones and the town has become the world's most important opal producing area. The opal fields cover nearly 5000 square kilometres, and there are around 250 000 mine shafts. Opal mining has grown to become a multimillion-dollar industry.

Tourism is an increasingly important industry in Coober Pedy. Around 100 000 tourists now visit the town each year. People come to see the unusual way of living, and are able to stay in underground hotels. Tourists have the chance to tour opal mines and to buy jewellery made in the town. Coober Pedy is also used as a setting for movies. *Mad Max 3* was shot there because of the town's harsh and rugged appearance.

Extract from a traveller's diary

Slowly in the distance the township began to emerge. Where on earth were we? Australia? It is difficult to describe how Coober Pedy looks as you are driving towards it but all I can say is that I honestly felt that I was no longer on earth. There is nothing. No tree, no grass, no buildings. All you can see are huge mounds of red dirt. My first sighting of Coober Pedy will always stay in my mind.

Change

Coober Pedy has changed a great deal since the 1960s.
- A tarmac road has been built through the centre of the town.
- More shops have opened.
- Mains water has been connected.

Although business in opals and tourism is doing well, there is little for the young people of Coober Pedy. There are no clubs, and the drive-in cinema has closed down. Young people are leaving Coober Pedy to find work in the towns and cities on Australia's coast.

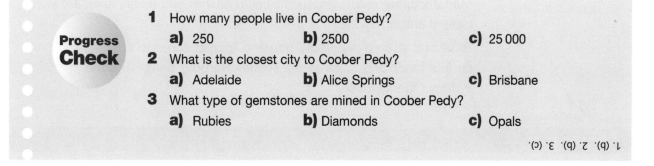

Progress Check

1 How many people live in Coober Pedy?
   a) 250   **b)** 2500   **c)** 25 000
2 What is the closest city to Coober Pedy?
   a) Adelaide   **b)** Alice Springs   **c)** Brisbane
3 What type of gemstones are mined in Coober Pedy?
   a) Rubies   **b)** Diamonds   **c)** Opals

1. (b). 2. (b). 3. (c).

11.7 Sydney

Key Point   Sydney is Australia's oldest, largest and most important city.

Sydney covers a huge area of 12 400 square kilometres.

Sydney is located on the south-eastern coast of Australia, and was the first place to be settled by the British.

Sydney's central business district (CBD) of shops and offices is on the southern shore of Sydney Harbour. It is a densely packed mixture of old colonial buildings and modern skyscrapers. Large areas of housing stretch out from the CBD.

Sydney's population is around 3.7 million people. The city is a popular destination for immigrants and there are a large number of people from Lebanon, Vietnam, Turkey, China, Italy and Greece.

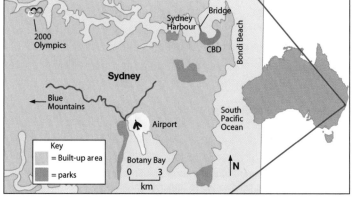

Fig. 11.7 Location of Sydney.

Environment

Sydney has grown into an important city because of its excellent location and pleasant environment. It is bordered to the west by the Blue Mountains, to the north by the Hawkesbury River, and by the Southern Highlands to the south.

The city has a comfortable climate with low rainfall spread fairly evenly throughout the year. The average summer temperature is 27°C, and even in the winter it is a warm 17°C.

Economy

Sydney is Australia's most important commercial centre. Over 60 large companies have their headquarters in the city, providing many office jobs. Manufacturing industries, such as oil refineries and textile mills, are also located around Sydney.

Tourism is also an important industry. Tourists come to see famous landmarks, such as the Sydney Harbour Bridge and the Sydney Opera House.

Change

Sydney is a popular place to live but it has no more room to expand. This has caused house prices to rise, forcing people to move further into the suburbs, where houses are cheaper. Traditionally, Australian houses have been single-storey buildings with large gardens. Today, in some places these are being knocked down and replaced with blocks of flats.

Sydney was the site for the 2000 Olympic Games. Although this brought benefits, it also increased pressure on the city. The site of the main Olympic stadium was a highly polluted industrial wasteland. This area was cleaned up and is now safe. The Olympics also created many jobs in construction, tourism and catering. However, local facilities were closed down to make space for Olympic buildings. Traffic congestion also became worse as road layouts were changed.

Progress Check

1 Where is Sydney located?
2 Describe Sydney's CBD.
3 What is the population of Sydney?
4 Describe Sydney's climate.
5 What event in 2000 brought change to Sydney?

1. South-eastern Australia. 2. Mixture of old colonial buildings and modern skyscrapers. 3. 3.7 million. 4. Low rainfall spread throughout year. Average summer temperature 27°C, average winter temperature 17°C. 5. The Olympic Games.

Practice questions

1 Name features **a** – **e** on the map of Australia. **(5)**

2 Why do most Australians live near the coast? **(2)**

3 From which of the following countries have large numbers of people migrated to Australia? **(5)**

Canada
Britain
Brazil
USA
Greece
Italy
Vietnam
Denmark
Malaysia
Kenya

12 Brazil

The topics covered in this chapter are:

- Physical geography
- Population and settlement
- Development
- Agriculture and industry
- Deforestation
- Rio de Janeiro

After studying this topic you should be able to:

- locate Brazil
- describe Brazil's rivers, relief, climates and ecosystems
- describe and explain the distribution of population, settlement, employment and quality of life
- recognise different indicators of development and know how to apply them to Brazil
- understand life in rural areas of Brazil
- describe and explain the processes that have shaped Brazil
- evaluate the impact people are having on Brazil's ecosystems
- understand life in urban areas in Brazil.

12.1 Physical geography

Key Point

Brazil is the largest country in South America. It is found between the latitude lines 5° north and 33° south, and the longitude lines 74° west and 35° east.

The name Amazon comes from the Indian word Amossona, which means 'wrecker of boats'.

Brazil's main river is the Amazon, the second longest river in the world at 6570 km. Other rivers include the Parana and the São Francisco. The Brazilian Highlands are found in the south-east of Brazil. In the centre of the country is a plateau called the Mato Grosso. In the north is the Amazon river basin.

Fig. 12.1 The location of Brazil.

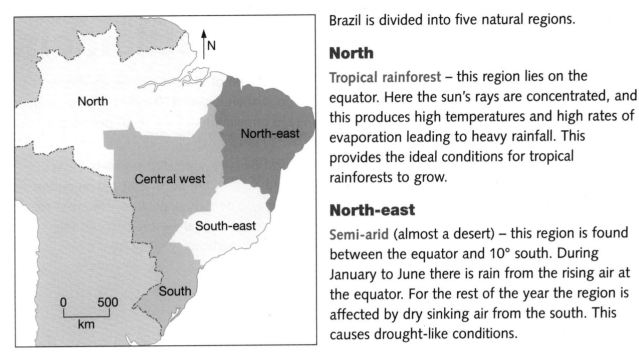

Fig. 12.2 Brazil's regions.

Brazil is divided into five natural regions.

North

Tropical rainforest – this region lies on the equator. Here the sun's rays are concentrated, and this produces high temperatures and high rates of evaporation leading to heavy rainfall. This provides the ideal conditions for tropical rainforests to grow.

North-east

Semi-arid (almost a desert) – this region is found between the equator and 10° south. During January to June there is rain from the rising air at the equator. For the rest of the year the region is affected by dry sinking air from the south. This causes drought-like conditions.

Central west

Tropical grassland – this region is found between 10° and 20° south. Temperatures are high all year and there is a wet and a dry season. There is sufficient rainfall for tropical grasslands to flourish.

South-east

Subtropical forest – this region is between 20° and 30° south. The temperatures are cooler than at the equator and there is high rainfall throughout the year. This provides perfect growing conditions for palm trees and other subtropical plants.

South

Temperate grassland and forest – this is between 25° and 35° south. The climate here is relatively similar to the south of the UK – it is quite wet, the temperature varies between 10° and 25°C, and it falls as low as freezing on some occasions. Here the vegetation is deciduous trees and shrubs.

Progress Check

Match the descriptions to the words below.
1 The capital city of Brazil.
2 The largest city in Brazil (18 million inhabitants).
3 A river in the east of Brazil.
4 A country to the west of Brazil.
5 An ocean to the east of Brazil.

Peru   Atlantic   São Francisco   Brasilia   São Paulo

1. Brasilia. 2. São Paulo. 3. São Francisco. 4. Peru. 5. Atlantic.

12.2 Population and settlement

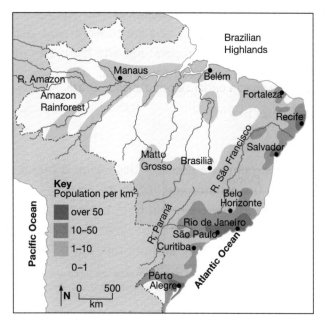

Fig. 12.3 Population distribution.

The population of Brazil is not evenly distributed. The population is over 170 million people, with an average population density of 20 people per square kilometre.

The most densely populated region is the south-east, and parts of the north-east region on the coast are also densely populated. The most sparse regions are the central west region and the north region, particularly away from main transport routes.

> **Key Point**
>
> The distribution of population can be explained by looking at the history and physical geography of Brazil.

Large parts of Brazil have a population density of less than 1 person per square kilometre.

In 1500 Brazil became a Portuguese colony. The main transport between the two countries was by sea so the coastal parts of Brazil became the first to develop. Sugar plantations were established on the coast in the north-east, settlements were established and Salvador became the capital city.

The parts of the country closest to the coast still have the greatest concentrations of people. This is where the main cities are located: Recife, Salvador, Rio de Janeiro, São Paulo, Belo Horizonte and Curitaba. Even though some of these cities are not directly on the coast, their proximity to the coast has been essential for their growth.

Coffee was introduced to Brazil during the early 16th century. It grew well in the climate of the south-east. The wealth produced by the trade in coffee encouraged many people to live there. In 1763 Rio de Janeiro took over as the capital city.

In the early 20th century industry began to develop in the south-east. This included food processing, iron and steel production and engineering. São Paulo became a major industrial centre by 1920. This encouraged more people to move to this region.

In the early 1960s a new city called Brasilia was built in the central west region. This became the new capital of Brazil. It was intended to draw economic development and people away from the coast and into the interior of the country.

The north has a sparse population density because of its location and accessibility. It is over 1000 km from the south-east coast of Brazil.

The landscape consists of dense tropical rainforest, which makes development difficult. For years there were few roads or settlements, and the population consisted of indigenous Amazonian Indian tribes.

12.3 Development

Brazil	Indicator	UK
0.739	HDI	0.923
$6500	GDP per capita	$22 000
172.6 million	Population	59.5 million
1.7%	Population growth rate	0.1%
68	Life expectancy	78
81%	Percentage urban	90%
23%	Percentage working in agriculture	2%
85%	Adult literacy	99%
20	Birth rate	13
9	Death rate	11
32	Infant mortality rate	6

South-east Brazil	Indicator	North-east Brazil
67.7 million	Population	48.3 million
22	Birth rate	48
49	Infant mortality rate	109
63	Life expectancy	48
72	Adult literacy	39
64%	Share of national wealth	14%
70%	Percentage employed in industry	10%
64%	Percentage with clean water	23%

The development of Brazil can be measured using a range of indicators. By putting the same indicators for the UK alongside you will be able to compare the differences in development between the two countries.

However, these are national figures. If you compare figures for the south-east and the north-east of Brazil you will see that the levels of development in the two regions are not the same.

As you can see, the south-east of Brazil is more developed than the north-east. You would expect this because the south-east is the wealthiest region, with most jobs and cities. If you were to find figures for the north region, you would expect the difference to be even greater.

12.4 Agriculture

The indigenous people from the Amazon rainforest are known as Amerindians. Groups of Amerindians include the Kayapo, the Tukano and the Yanomami.

Agriculture in Brazil is a mixture of smallholdings farmed by individual farmers, large estates owned by landowners and farmed by labourers, and traditional farming by Amerindians in the Amazon rainforest.

Smallholdings are relatively rare in Brazil. The government has created a scheme to encourage people to move to the north region to set up farms. The settlers are given free land, up to 100 hectares, which they must clear themselves before they begin farming.

Some farmers harvest Brazil nuts from trees which they plant amongst the rainforest trees. They are able to make a profit from this type of farming and it is sustainable because the rainforest is not destroyed.

Most of the farming in Brazil is extensive commercial farming on **large estates** of cash crops, mainly sugar cane and coffee. Other estates are cattle ranches. Farms can be 50 000 hectares in area, 300 times larger than the average farm in the UK. Many of the landowners are the descendants of Portuguese settlers or farm labourers.

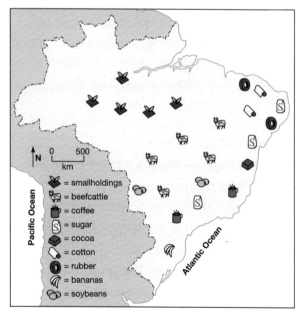

Fig. 12.4 Agriculture.

Sugar cane grows particularly well in the climates of the north-east and south-east regions. About 40 per cent of the sugar cane is exported, the rest is turned into alcohol to fuel cars. One third of the sugar cane is harvested by hand, the rest is done by machinery. Work is hard – labourers work from 7am to 5pm, work isn't guaranteed and most people have contracts that last for only one day.

Ranching is found in the central west and north regions. Ranching is responsible for 40 per cent of the land cleared in the Amazon rainforest. Vast areas have been cleared in order to provide grazing land for beef cattle. Originally the beef was sold to North America for fast food hamburgers, but following protests from the public this has stopped.

Shifting cultivation is a type of agriculture that is practised by the indigenous people of the tropical rainforests. Technically it is classified as extensive subsistence nomadic agriculture.

Shifting cultivation involves four stages.

- An area of about a hectare of rainforest is cleared. Machetes are used and the area is set on fire to release the nutrients from the felled trees. This is known as 'slash and burn'.
- Crops such as manioc, yams, beans and pumpkins are planted.
- The area is farmed for four or five years until the soil begins to lose its fertility, then the Amerindians move to a new area.
- It takes about 50 years for the rainforest to grow back once it has been cleared in this way, but the rainforest does recover and is not destroyed completely.

> Manioc is a bit like a potato. The roots of the plant contain starch, which is used to make a form of tapioca or bread.

Progress Check

1 Where are most smallholdings found in Brazil?
2 How can the smallholdings be farmed sustainably?
3 Which crops are grown on the large estates?
4 Why is shifting cultivation also known as slash and burn?
5 Does shifting cultivation destroy the rainforest?

1. In the north. 2. Because crops can be grown on the forest floor without cutting down the trees.
3. Coffee and sugar. 4. Because the farmers slash the forest with machetes, then set fire to it.
5. No, the forest will grow back, but only if it left for 50 years.

12.5 Industry

Brazil has the ninth largest economy in the world. It is also the ninth largest manufacturer of cars.

Key Point

Brazil's main industries are food processing, vehicle assembly, computer manufacture and electronics.

> Bauxite is used to make aluminium.

> Many of Brazil's major employers are foreign-owned companies who have moved to Brazil to take advantage of the cheap labour there.

> An alternative to paying back with money is 'debt for nature swaps', where debt is cancelled in return for Brazil protecting its precious ecosystems such as the Amazon rainforest.

Brazil has an abundance of natural resources which will make future industrial growth possible. These include gold, diamonds, oil, iron ore and bauxite. There are large areas of the country that have not been opened up for people so there is plenty of room to expand industry – 90 per cent of the population live on 25 per cent of the land. Brazil also has large fast-flowing rivers to provide hydroelectricity – currently Brazil generates 91 per cent of its electricity in this way.

Brazil began its industrial development at the start of the 20th century. In the 1960s and 1970s Brazil's growth was described as an economic miracle, when the economy was growing at a rate of 10 per cent a year. However, the government had borrowed a lot of money to help the industry to grow and Brazil now has debts of $112 billion to pay back. At the moment Brazil is having to use a third of the money it makes from selling goods to other countries to pay back its debts.

Brazil is saving money by reducing the amount of oil that it buys from other countries. Many cars in Brazil run on alcohol so the country does not need to import as much oil. The alcohol is made from sugar cane which is grown in Brazil. This is an environmentally sustainable scheme because fossil fuels are being conserved, and sugar cane alcohol is renewable. In addition, the waste materials from the alcohol production are burnt to generate electricity.

Iron and steel in Brazil

Iron ore was discovered in the Amazon rainforest at a site called Carajas. There are 18 billion tonnes of iron ore there, enough to last for 400 years. It has cost the Brazilian government £2 billion to develop an iron ore mine at Carajas – the biggest in the world, employing 7000 people and making up 8 per cent of the iron ore that is sold around the world.

Despite the mine being in the middle of the rainforest only 1.6 per cent of the trees have been cut down, as a result of careful planning. A brand new town has been built to house the workers. Rents are low, there is free healthcare, fresh food, swimming pools, a good education system and a safe environment.

Energy comes from the Tucurui HEP dam on the Tocantins river. The iron ore is taken to the coast where it is exported to countries such as Japan, Korea and Germany.

Tourism

There were 5.31 million visitors to Brazil in 2000. They are attracted by over 1000 miles of beaches, the natural beauty of the Amazon tropical rainforest and the nightlife of cities such as Rio de Janeiro. Some 2.5 per cent of Brazil's income is generated by tourism, but this is low compared to the world average of 10 per cent. Brazil is planning to improve its tourist facilities to attract more holidaymakers in the future.

Progress Check

Choose your answers from these numbers.

10   91   112   9   1000

1 Where does Brazil's economy come in relation to the rest of the world (if the biggest is 1st)?

2 What is the percentage of Brazil's energy that is generated by HEP?

3 What was the growth rate of Brazil's economy in the 1960s and 70s?

4 What is the amount of Brazil's debt?

5 How many miles of beaches are there in Brazil?

1. 9th. 2. 91 per cent. 3. 10 per cent. 4. $112 billion. 5. 1000.

12.6 Deforestation

The Amazon contains two fifths of the world's tropical rainforest, one third of the world's trees.

The Amazon has been described as a 'gene bank'. This means that it contains the genetic information of countless species. Rainforests have already provided us with foods such as rice, potatoes, tomatoes, peanuts and Brazil nuts. They are also an important source of medicines – e.g. quinine, which prevents malaria, and a flower called the rosy periwinkle, which has been used to combat leukaemia.

One 10km square of the Amazon contains:

- 1500 species of flowering plants
- 750 species of trees
- 400 species of birds
- 150 species of butterfly
- 100 species of reptiles

> Since the use of the periwinkle began, deaths from leukaemia have fallen by 60 per cent.

> The potential value of the Amazon for food and medicine has been calculated at $2000 billion.

However, the Amazon tropical rainforest is being cut down at an alarming rate. In 1970 it was still 99 per cent intact. Between 1970 and 2000, 20 per cent of the rainforest was cleared. This is the equivalent of an area the size of England and Wales every year, 15 hectares a minute, or one hectare every four seconds.

Key Point

If deforestation is not controlled only 28 per cent of the Amazon rainforest will be left by 2020.

> It is estimated that 100 000 species will become extinct in the next 40 years as a result of deforestation. The potential for discovering new foods or medicines from these species will be lost forever.

The tragedy is that the rainforest does not grow back. This is because most of the nutrients which the plants need to grow are stored in the trees. Once the trees have been removed, the source of the nutrients disappears. Any goodness that is left in the soil is quickly washed away by the heavy rainfall that happens in this region.

There used to be 6 million indigenous people in the Amazon rainforest; today there are only 200 000 left. This is because deforestation is destroying their traditional lands, they have suffered from disease brought in by settlers to which they have no immunity, and they have suffered massacres by people wanting to take their land. It is not just cultures which have existed for thousands of years that are disappearing, but knowledge of the rainforest and its plants which could give vital information for medical and food use.

Why is the Amazon being destroyed?

Agriculture: the forest has been cleared to create farmland for large estates.

Settlement: trees have been cut down to open the North region to settlers.

Ranching: a major cause of deforestation is for beef cattle farming.

Logging: rainforest wood is particularly hard and long lasting – one variety is mahogany which is mainly exported to make furniture.

Mining: the Amazon is rich in minerals such as iron ore, tin and gold – the forest is destroyed by the mines.

Dams: Brazil plans to build 73 dams in the Amazon region. The dams provide essential electricity, which is a renewable energy source. However, the forest is flooded and wildlife lose their habitat.

Roads: 12 000 km of roads have been built in the Amazon.

Attempts to reduce deforestation

The Brazilian government has tried to reduce the amount of deforestation in various ways.

- In 1989 a scheme to encourage people to develop the rainforest was cancelled.
- In 1996 no more licences to cut down trees for mahogany were given.
- Satellite monitoring is being used to identify parts of the forest that are being cleared illegally.
- A number of national parks have been created.
- Sustainable uses of the forest are being promoted, where money can be made from the forest without destroying it.
- Ecotourism is being developed so that money can be made from the forest through wildlife tours and conservation holidays.

Ecotourism works because the greater the level of protection of the forest the better the quality of the experience for the tourists, so conservation is made a priority.

Examples of sustainable uses of the forest include sustainable logging, where trees that are cut down are replaced by new ones and agro-forestry, where farmers grow crops on the forest floor without cutting down any trees.

We can help to protect the rainforest by making sure that we do not buy any products that are responsible for trees being cut down. Most wood products today carry a sustainable forestry mark so that you know that trees are planted to replace any trees that are cut down. We can also support organisations that campaign to protect rainforests such as Friends of the Earth or Greenpeace.

Progress Check

1 Name three foods that we get from tropical rainforests.

2 Name one disease that can be treated or prevented using plants from tropical rainforests.

3 How much of the Amazon rainforest could be destroyed by 2020?

4 What are the main causes of the deforestation?

5 Why won't the forest grow back?

1. Tomatoes, peanuts, Brazil nuts, potatoes, rice. 2. Malaria, leukaemia. 3. 72 per cent. 4. Agriculture, settlement, ranching, logging, mining, dams and roads. 5. Because the nutrients needed are stored in the trees, and erosion results. When the trees are cleared nutrients needed are washed away.

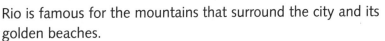

12.7 Rio de Janeiro

Rio de Janeiro is the second largest city in Brazil, with a population of over 10 million people and an area of 6500 square kilometres. Rio de Janeiro developed as a port for exporting products such as sugar and coffee and importing goods from the rest of the world.

Fig. 12.5 Rio.

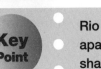

Rio is famous for the mountains that surround the city and its golden beaches.

A travel brochure describes Rio in this way:

A unique combination of spectacular sightseeing including Sugar Loaf mountain with the statue of Christ the Redeemer at its peak, sunkissed beaches such as the Copacabana, fabulous entertainment and outstanding natural beauty.

Key Point

Rio de Janeiro is a city of contrasts: skyscrapers, wealthy apartment blocks, expensive shops and hotels adjacent to shanty towns, poverty, unemployment and crime.

Rio de Janeiro means 'river of January'. Some people think it is named after the arrival of Portuguese explorers on 1 January 1502, but there is no river that runs through Rio!

One third of the population of Rio de Janeiro live in shanty towns known as **favelas**. An example of this is a favela known as Rocinha. Rocinha began as a collection of wooden shacks built on a steep slope on the edge of Rio de Janeiro. It was unplanned, and had no electricity, running water or sewerage system. Today 1 million people live there, the wooden shacks have been converted into brick-built homes and the area has been connected to the water, electricity and sewerage systems. There are shops, schools, entertainment and 25 channels on satellite TV.

Rio de Janeiro has become overcrowded, as immigrants are continually arriving in the city in search of a better life than in the countryside. There is no room left to build housing and services, and there is severe traffic congestion and high levels of pollution.

15 years ago the Brazilian government built Barra, a new town along the coast, connected by motorway to Rio de Janeiro. Its population is 130 000, and it has shops, entertainment, a 5-km-long shopping mall and European-style homes and apartments. It has been described as the California of Brazil. Residents there prefer it to Rio de Janeiro because the quality of life is much better – there is less crime, pollution, noise and traffic congestion.

Progress Check

Decide whether these phrases describe, Rio de Janeiro, Rocinha or Barra.
1 On a steep slope.
2 Polluted, noisy, over-crowded.
3 The California of Brazil.
4 Built 15 years ago.
5 Unplanned.
6 Sunkissed beaches such as Copacabana.

1. Rocinha. 2. Rio de Janeiro. 3. Barra. 4. Barra. 5. Rocinha. 6. Rio de Janeiro.

Practice questions

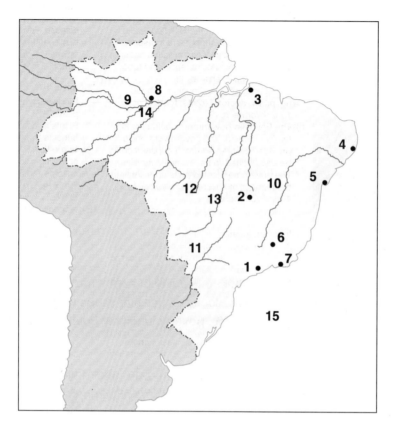

1 With the help of an atlas, show the physical and human features of Brazil by matching the numbers with the labels below. **(15)**

Human	**Physical**
Recife	Atlantic ocean
Brasilia	São Francisco river
Belo Horizonte	Amazon rainforest
São Paulo	Matto Grosso
Manaus	Brazilian Highlands
Belèm	Paranà river
Rio de Janeiro	Amazon river
Salvador	

2 Why are most of the cities found near the coast? **(3)**

3 Give one argument for and one argument against developing more settlements in the north of Brazil. **(2)**

Answers

Chapter 1
1 Ordnance Survey (1)
2 a) Church with a tower (1)
b) Main road (1)
c) Coniferous wood (1)
d) Post office (1)
e) Farm (1)
f) Information centre (1)
3 See page 12. (8)
4

(3)

5 A = 008214 (1)
  B = 022226 (1)
  C = 020204 (1)

Chapter 2
1 A = inner core, B = outer core,
  C = mantle, D = crust (4)
2 Jigsaw fit, identical fossils, matching
  mountain ranges, rock types. *1 mark for
  each of any 3.*
3 The Earth's core is hot due to radioactive
  processes (1); heat from the core rises
  into the mantle (1); convection currents in
  the mantle cause the semi-molten rock to
  move (1); mantle movements drag the
  tectonic plates sideways (1).
4 A = shield volcano, B = dome volcano, C
  = ash volcano, D = composite volcano (4)

Chapter 3
1 Sedimentary rocks are formed from other
  rocks (1), or the remains of living
  creatures (1).
2 (a), (d), (e), (c), (b) (5)
3 Abrasion, attrition, hydraulic action,
  plucking. *1 mark for each of any 3.*
4 A = watershed, B = source, C = tributary,
  D = confluence, E = mouth (5)
5 See diagram on page 47. (4)

Chapter 4
1 temperature = degrees Celsius (1)
  precipitation = millimetres (1)
  air pressure = millibars (1)
  wind speed = kilometres per hour (1)
  cloud cover = oktas (1)
2 A = convectional, B = frontal, C = relief (3)
3 Clear skies, hot, dry, still. (2)
4 Cloudy, cool, wet, windy. (2)
5 average temperature = hotter (1)
  average rainfall = wetter (1)
  average windspeed = slower (1)

Chapter 5
1 A = coniferous forest, B = temperate
  grassland, C = tropical rainforest,
  D = deciduous woodland, E = desert (5)
2 plankton → shrimp → penguin → seal →
  killer whale (5)
3 cactus = desert
  ash tree = deciduous woodland
  acacia tree = tropical grassland
  mahogany tree = tropical rainforest (4)
4 Agriculture, settlement, ranching, logging,
  mining, dams. *1 mark for each of any 3.*

Chapter 6
1 a) The population of Egypt is unevenly
  distributed. Most of the country is
  sparsely populated. The highest

population densities are found along the
course of the Nile. *1 mark for each.* (3)
b) People live close to the Nile because it
  provides a water supply and transport.
  People live on the Mediterranean coast
  because it provides transport and food.
  1 mark for each answer. (2)
2 a) Not enough jobs, housing, schools,
  hospitals, doctors, roads, food, space.
  1 mark for each. (2)
b) The Egyptian government could promote
  family planning. The government could
  provide free birth control. Egyptians could
  be encouraged to have smaller families.
  The government could pass laws limiting
  the number of children families can have.
  1 mark for each. (3)

Chapter 7
1 Its exact location. (1)
2 A = on a steep slope, B = on a hillside in a
  wood, C = on flat, fertile land, D = next to
  a river. *1 mark for each.* (4)
3 C is the best site because it is on flat and
  fertile land; it is near wood for building
  and fuel; it is near a water supply; it will
  not flood; it is not too steep to build on.
  1 mark for each. (4)
4 Sites like A and D are the sites that no
  one else wants; they can be flooded; they
  are steep which makes them difficult to
  build on; the land will be empty and
  cheap to buy or rent. *1 mark for each.* (4)

Chapter 8
1 Pastoral: sheep, too much rain, cold
  winters, hilly. (5)
  Arable: rich soil, flat, plenty of sun, wheat.
  (5)
2 In southern/central Scotland/between
  Glasgow and Edinburgh; north-east
  England/around Newcastle; along the M4
  motorway/from Newport to London/from
  London to Cambridge; south
  coast/around Southampton.
  1 mark for each. (4)
3 Easy transport along the motorway; easy
  to get to Heathrow airport; plenty of
  customers in nearby settlements; easy to
  get to Europe; near good universities;
  pleasant environment; greenfield sites;
  near research and development
  establishments. *1 mark for each.* (3)

Chapter 9
1 Income per person, adult literacy and life
  expectancy. *1 mark for each.* (3)
2 1 and 0. (2)
3 In Africa. (1)
4 North America, Europe, Japan, Australia
  and New Zealand. *1 mark for each.* (3)
5 Climate – extremes of climate make
  development difficult. Relief –
  mountainous landscapes inhibit
  development. Water supply – places
  which are arid or suffer frequent flooding
  have development problems. Ecosystems
  – dense forests make development
  difficult. Natural resources – a country
  with plenty of natural resources is at an
  economic advantage compared to a
  country that does not. Colonialism –
  stripped wealth from the colonised
  country and created an unfair system of
  employment and international trade. Civil
  war – money that could be spent on
  development is put into war. Debt –

LEDCs spend money paying back loans
rather than on development. Health and
disease – development in some countries
has been held back by the prevalence of
disease. *1 mark for the reason,
1 mark for an explanation, x 3.* (6)

Chapter 10
1 Biodiversity is the rich variety of life on the
  planet. (1)
2 Plants and living creatures could have
  benefits to people such as providing food
  or medicine. We don't know what effect
  changing one part of an ecosystem will
  have on the rest of an ecosystem or on
  the planet as a whole. Wildlife has a right
  to exist as much as humans; it is our
  responsibility to conserve wildlife rather
  than destroy it. *1 mark for each.* (3)
3 Burning fossil fuels destroys wildlife
  habitats by causing acid rain and global
  warming. Mining and forestry causes
  deforestation and the loss of habitats. Oil
  spills can destroy habitats on land and in
  the sea. *1 mark for each.* (3)
4 Alternative energy sources can be
  developed which don't pollute the
  environment. The land can be restored
  once the extraction of natural resources
  has been completed. Natural resource use
  can be sustainable, so that resources that
  can be replaced and only small areas are
  allowed to be affected at a time, so the
  environment has time to adapt and
  recover. *1 mark for each.* (3)

Chapter 11
1 A = Western Plateau, B = Central
  Lowlands, C = Eastern Highlands,
  D = Great Barrier Reef, E = Uluru (Ayer's
  Rock) (5)
2 Coastal locations have a temperate
  climate (1), trade with other countries (1).
3 Britain (1), Greece (1), Italy (1), Vietnam (1),
  Malaysia (1).

Chapter 12
1 1 mark for each correct location – see
  map on page 148. (15)
2 The coast was where the Portuguese first
  settled. Ports were established to import
  and export goods. Industry developed at
  the coast to take advantage of the ports.
  People were attracted to the industry for
  employment. The coastal regions have
  climates which are favourable for growing
  crops such as cocoa, coffee and sugar.
  The rest of Brazil is more
  remote/inaccessible/has fewer jobs/has a
  climate that is less favourable for
  agriculture. *1 mark for each.* (3)
3 Arguments for: relieves overcrowding and
  pressure at the coast; provides jobs and a
  better quality of life in the north; enables
  Brazil to take advantage of natural
  resources in the north such as timber, iron
  ore and HEP. 1 mark for any of these.
  Arguments against: settlement in the north
  destroys the tropical rain forest;
  biodiversity is lost which could provide
  food and medicine in the future;
  deforestation contributes to global
  warming; indigenous groups (Amerindians)
  lose their traditional lands. *1 mark for any
  of these.* (2)

Index

Acknowledgements

The author and publisher are grateful to the copyright holders, as credited, for permission to use quoted materials and photographs.

Energy Efficiency: Fig 10.8; James Davies Travel Photography: 5.5, 5.6 & 12.5; Philips Publishing: Fig 1.3; specialist publishing services (photography) ltd: pages 22 & 110, Figs 3.3 (Liz Draper), 5.3, 7.2 (Martin Skelton) & 10.6. This publication includes mapping and symbols from Ordnance Survey® with the permission of the Controller of her Majesty's Stationery Office, © Crown copyright. All rights reserved. Licence no. 1000/17272. The symbols in this publication may be used for educational purposes only.

Every effort has been made to trace the copyright holders and to obtain their permission for the use of copyright material. The author and publisher will gladly receive information enabling them to rectify any error or omission in subsequent editions.

Letts Educational
4 Grosvenor Place
London
SW1X 7DL

School enquiries: 01539 564910
Parent & student enquiries: 01539 564913
E-mail: mail@lettsed.co.uk
Website: www.letts-educational.com

First published 2004

Revised Edition 2007

Text © Adam Arnell and Andy Browne 2004

British Library Cataloging in Publication Data. A CIP record of this book is available from the British Library.

ISBN 978 1 84315 273 6

Prepared by *specialist* publishing services ltd, Milton Keynes

Printed in Dubai